FOREIGN
INVESTMENT
AND DEVELOPMENT
IN EGYPT

FOREIGN INVESTMENT AND DEVELOPMENT IN EGYPT

DAVID WILLIAM CARR

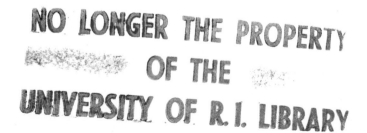

PRAEGER PUBLISHERS
Praeger Special Studies

New York   •   London   •   Sydney   •   Toronto

Library of Congress Cataloging in Publication Data

Carr, David William, 1936–
    Foreign investment and development in Egypt.

    Bibliography: p.
    Includes index.
    1. Investments, Foreign--Egypt. 2. Egypt--Economic
conditions--1952-   I. Title.
HG5836.A3C37   332.6'73'0962   79-1230
ISBN 0-03-048351-4

PRAEGER PUBLISHERS, PRAEGER SPECIAL STUDIES
383 Madison Avenue, New York, N.Y., 10017, U.S.A.

Published in the United States of America in 1979
by Praeger Publishers,
A Division of Holt, Rinehart and Winston, CBS Inc.

9 038 987654321

Printed in the United States of America

ACKNOWLEDGMENTS

During the preparation of this book, I have benefited greatly from contacts with government officials representing the United States and Egypt, as well as U.S. businessmen active in Egypt. I am indebted to James Roberts, Egypt Desk Officer of the Agency for International Development, for supplying me with much recent information on developments in the industries and the financial situation of Egypt. Dr. Ibrahim Oweiss, Director of the Egyptian Economic Mission in New York, and Gamal el Nazar, Egyptian Minister of State for Economic Affairs and Economic Cooperation, during a seminar sponsored by the National Foreign Trade Council on September 29, 1978, provided many helpful insights on the foreign investment climate in their country. The Council president, Robert M. Norris, and the vice president, Richard W. Roberts, have given me valuable help and advice during the preparatory work for this and other meetings of U.S. business executives and foreign government officials for the exchange of views on foreign investment problems and opportunities.

I wish to thank John Brewer, executive director of the Egypt-U.S. Business Council, for his helpful comments on the Egyptian experiences of some American investors and on some aspects of the general business environment. I should also like to thank Robert Hawkins, professor of economics and chairman of the Department of International Business at the Graduate School of Business Administration of New York University, for his assistance in the task of refining the theoretical framework presented in Chapter 1.

I would like to give special thanks to my secretary at the Council, Anita Favini, who not only typed the manuscript but offered many helpful suggestions regarding inconsistencies in the texts and tables.

For lending me encouragement along the way during a busy period, I must extend gratitude to my wife, Kate, and our children, Cynthia, Elizabeth, and Christopher.

CONTENTS

LIST OF TABLES AND FIGURE

1

ANALYTICAL FRAMEWORK

Since 1973, Egypt has received a good deal of attention from financial and business leaders in the Middle East, the Western countries, and the international community. This attention appears to be derived from Egypt's forceful actions toward resolving its international and domestic problems. Many people consider that Egypt is in a "turn-around" situation and that, in contrast to the previous stagnation, much progress is now taking place.

Egypt is strategically placed to attract continuing attention. As a result of the five-fold increase in petroleum prices during 1973–74, the Middle East region acquired tremendous wealth and a surplus of investable funds. Egypt has a fairly large domestic market of 40 million persons and is adjacent to the markets of the Middle East, Africa, and Europe. The country has a large labor force with extensive skills, together with fairly good infrastructural facilities. The steady liberalization of government controls and the steps being taken to remove other constraints on vigorous business activity are also major attractions.

Many foreign investors have been investigating opportunities in the Egyptian market which would yield reasonable profits for them, and, at the same time, contribute to Egypt's development goals. This book is an attempt to appraise the overall potential for mutually fruitful relationships between foreign investors and Egyptian private and public firms.

A full appreciation of the potential impact of foreign direct investment in promoting the growth of a developing country such as Egypt can best be obtained through a dynamic analysis. The first section of this book accordingly presents the essential elements of the dynamic view of foreign trade or investment, stressing the contention that high net benefits are most likely to arise with vigorous reactions by host entities.

The second section analyzes in detail the technology transfer mechanism and describes how the various returns from direct investment originate. With

1

the industrial organization approach, the returns are attributable to the transfer and dissemination of the special assets possessed by foreign investors. In the main, these special assets consist of a continuing stream of new knowledge, products, or processes, and the host country benefits through their widespread transmission.

An outline of the major issues dealt with in this book is presented in the concluding section of this chapter. An underlying theme of the past and prospective Egyptian experiences with foreign investment is the fact that the best contributions to Egyptian growth are obtainable when the Egyptians themselves act vigorously while enjoying cooperative relationships with foreign enterprises, and when foreign investors participate in many significant projects while avoiding a position of dominance.

THE THEORETICAL FRAMEWORK—A DYNAMIC TRADE THEORY

This study on the role of foreign direct investment in the economic growth of Egypt is set within a dynamic framework. According to the doctrine of static comparative advantage, trade confers gains through international specialization and the resulting improvements in the efficiency of resource allocation. In a remarkable burst of insight forty years ago, Robertson observed that trade in the nineteenth century was not simply a device for the optimum allocation of a given stock of resources but, above all, it was an engine or transmitter of growth from important countries to peripheral areas.[1] In an analogous way, direct foreign investment has the potential to act as a growth engine for host countries.

In a series of essays, Ragnar Nurkse has elaborated the implications of this dynamic view.[2] Issawi's comments have also been enlightening.[3] Nurkse argued that it is essential to relax the assumption of constant factor supplies in the classical model of international trade. Rather, a host country's stock of productive factors should be portrayed as subject to change through growth in the labor force, improvements in education and skills, and the creation or importation of capital and technology. Nurkse argued that trade in the nineteenth century acted as an engine of growth for the less industrialized countries as Europe's growing demand for primary products initiated mutually reinforcing chains of favorable developments that led to higher capital investment, the stimulation of consumption demand, and more fruitful employment of resources in the less advanced areas. A flow of new productive factors was generated, as previously idle or lethargic resources were stirred up and worker skills were upgraded.

The crucial point in this dynamic view is the responsiveness of host entities to the external stimuli. According to the Issawi metaphor, foreign trade is the engine that provides the motive power, but this engine cannot move the host economy unless there are adequate transmission lines connecting the different sectors. Economic development is retarded if the export sector fails to transmit productivity improvements and a creative spirit to other sectors.

The analysis attempted in this study on the developmental impact of foreign direct investment uses the basic linkages of this dynamic view. In this view, the responsiveness and creativity of host institutions influence the benefits received through foreign investment activities. The gains to the host economy arise both from the use of additional factor resources imported from an advanced country and from the generation or improvement of additional resources within the host country. The developmental impact can be minimal, however, if there is little transmission of higher productivity to other sectors, if there are undesirable side effects, or if the creative efforts of local entities are stifled rather than stimulated. In accord with Nurkse's analysis of dynamic trade theory, high net benefits are most likely to arise and become reinforcing and cumulative when the reactions in the host country are the most vigorous. If reactions are sluggish or creativity is stifled, growth will be of the enclave type with little improvement in overall productivity.

Direct investment is taken to mean investment in operationally linked subsidiaries or affiliates as contrasted to portfolio investment, which is investment in equity and debt securities through the medium of an impersonal capital market. Direct investment entails control over the operations of the host-country firm through the provision of capital, technology, entrepreneurship, and access to markets as a package instead of their being made available separately through the marketplace. For example, many government officials deem direct investment to have taken place when investment is made through a branch of an overseas company or when there is ownership of 25 percent or more of a local company's voting stock by one company or a group of companies incorporated in an overseas country, or when there is a 50 percent private overseas ownership in general. The line is, of course, arbitrary and there may be cases where control can be secured with a smaller proportion of equity contribution through the use of the exceptionally complex technology that is constantly evolving.

THE TECHNOLOGY TRANSFER MECHANISM AND THE DERIVATION OF RETURNS

The Creation of Direct Investment Returns

Foreign direct investment is undertaken by investors and is accepted by host countries because of the shared belief that substantial returns are available from direct investment operations. According to the now dominant industrial organization approach to direct investment advanced notably by Hymer, Caves, Johnson, and Reddaway, these returns are attributable to the transfer and exploitation of special assets possessed by foreign investors.[4] The returns have a scarcity value and are linked to production in the host country and the special market circumstances there, with the transfer of technology or know-how taking place more efficiently or quickly through direct investment than through such alternative channels as embodiment in imports, licensing, consulting arrangements, or local generation. From the viewpoint of the foreign investor, the returns attributable to the special asset must be high enough to offset the excess costs of production in an alien location, such as adjusting to different economic, social, legal, and cultural conditions. From the viewpoint of a host country, the cost of adapting foreign technology to the host country must be less than the local costs of developing similar technology, and the net benefits greater, than seeking the technology through the other alternative mechanisms. The range of effective alternatives rises with the maturity of the host country's economy and technical capacity; at the early stages, the options are restricted. The size of the total returns over a long-term planning horizon depends importantly upon the differential value of the know-how transferred through direct investment as compared with the alternatives and taking into consideration adaptation and adjustment costs.[5] The growth effect on host countries is critically related to the effectiveness with which the new technology is absorbed and diffused, which is in turn dependent upon the responsiveness and creativity of local institutions.

The larger the minimum scale of the enterprise, and the greater the technological gap between the foreign firms and host, the more vital a direct investment relationship becomes with its on-the-spot management and technical involvement. A deficiency in such factors as engineers, technicians, and administrators would also make valuable an association with foreign investors.

In the extractive field, the differential returns from direct investment arise primarily from the faster discovery and exploitation of raw materials. A complete evaluation of the benefits from foreign investments in the extractive field depends, however, not merely upon an appraisal of the time saved through applying the foreign technology but also on price developments in the period during which foreign investments help to exploit a mineral deposit, this again being compared with the later period during which the deposit would have been exploited in the absence of foreign investment.

The returns to the foreign investor are principally in the form of dividends, technical fees, any unusual profits received from the sale of raw materials and components to the local affiliates, and capital appreciation above the normal rate of inflation. The returns to host entities may comprise higher productive capacities, higher wages, income, and employment, lower prices, a more competitive market structure, higher taxes, more exports, a diffusion of skills, improved efficiency of production in foreign affiliates and throughout industry, and the gradual spread of an enterprising spirit and technical and innovational capacities. On the other hand, direct investment operations can involve a long-term relationship of dependence on foreign firms. Many critics allege that this external dominance may have such costly effects as a possible stifling of the development of special skills and of R&D activity, the use of inappropriate scale technology, excessive importation, and biased transfer pricing. Other possible undesirable features, particularly if there is an oligopolistic market structure or excessive entry inducements, are diseconomies of scale, high prices, and export franchises.

For a visual impression of the various effects of foreign direct investment, see Figure 1.1.

The Nature of the Special Assets of Foreign Investors

The returns from direct investment arise from the addition of external resources, the more complete utilization of local resources, an upgrading in factor quality, and/or superior allocation or productivity in resource use. The specific assets transferred by foreign investors to host country entities comprise first of all proprietary know-how and special technical and managerial skills. The proprietary know-how and special skills refer primarily to new product and process technology and embrace product designs and formulas, and production and extraction techniques.[6]

Other important features of much direct investment are superior marketing and organizational connections and entrepreneurial ability. Recently, the focus has been on the giant multinational corporations, with their access to abundant information, and with their ability to mobilize financial, physical, and human resources around the globe and coordinate them in the various stages of production and marketing. Ideally, the returns from such activities accrue from economies of scale, the spreading of risks, rapid communications, worldwide marketing connections, access to diverse sources of knowledge and technology, and the concentration of decision making. Such negative features as the creation of inappropriate tastes and the distortion of local employment patterns have also been cited in the general literature, but appear to be largely absent from the Egyptian scene.[7]

A beneficial system for the transfer of know-how through direct investment would include the following three elements: 1) the know-how is closely held and lasts for some time before imitation and diffusion; 2) the technology consists of a continuing stream of new knowledge, products, or processes, not just a one-time transfer; and 3) the know-how comprises not merely the original technology or know-how but includes even more importantly the ability to use it efficiently.

FIGURE 1.1: Effects of Foreign Direct Investment

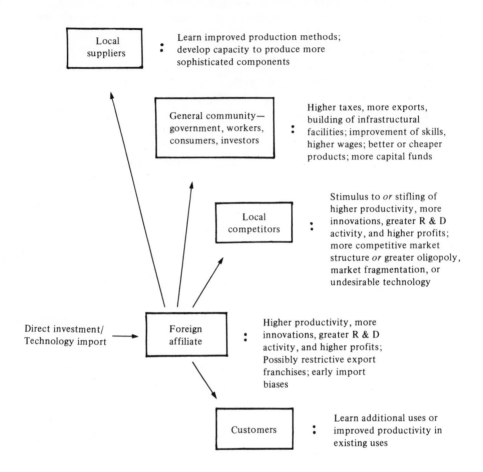

Source: David William Carr, "The Impact of Foreign Direct Investment on the Economic Development of Australia" (Ph.D. diss., New York University, 1979).

The ability of local firms to secure know-how through alternative methods depends first of all on whether similar know-how is possessed by a large number of other firms and secondly on whether the direct investment package is divisible. Wide product and process differentiation through secret formulas or patented designs and the inseparability of essential skills argue for the transfer of know-how through foreign equity participation.[8]

A direct investment relationship also implies direct and continuous ties with the parent companies. Access is thereby afforded to new technological developments emanating from the parent's research, and a stream of product and process improvements can flow. Mikesell states cogently that if technicians and managers are on hire, they take with them only the existing and later out-dated knowledge, whereas under direct investment, there is a growing fund of foreign company experience and research, from which to draw.

The final important aspect of the transfer of know-how through direct investment is the host country's ability to use it efficiently. Only a small part of technical know-how is codified in nonpersonal means of communications, such as technical manuals, process sheets, and new equipment. Much know-how is transferred by demonstration and training during the initial operations and thus frequently requires a sustained and close relationship among managers, engineering personnel, and workers.[9] The close relationships which develop between parents and subsidiaries are believed to result in a freer and more effective flow of information. The occasional problems of suddenly collapsing productivity attendant upon a too rapid shift to local responsibilities under licensing or consulting arrangements would also be avoided. The foreign firms are more committed to the success of projects with direct investment than if they are merely selling the technology.[10]

The industrial organization approach to direct investment is closely related to the approach taken here. The foreign affiliate in the host country derives benefits through receiving and exploiting the skills, know-how, and the other special assets possessed by foreign investors. The host country receives wider benefits to the extent that there is a transmission of improved productivity to other sectors and there is a generation of additional skills and creativity throughout the economy.

We should bear in mind that, in foreign investment evaluation, we are not dealing with a fixed or limited amount of net benefit to be divided between the investor and the host country and then among the various host entities. Most of the possible interactions in the flow of benefits from foreign investment can be more appropriately considered as partnership activities than games of competition. The idea that whatever one entity gains the other entity loses (or fails to gain) under distribution mechanics is not appropriate in the dynamic growth process underlying foreign investment. In many situations, creative enterprise in one sector or by one entity is like a fire which can inflame greater efforts, productivity, and skills nearby. A gain from growth stimulation in one sector can, in synergistic fashion, contribute to accelerated gains in many other sectors. Conversely, sluggish or defective reactions in one area can stifle creativity elsewhere.

AN OUTLINE OF MAJOR ISSUES

The focus of this book, dealing with the role of foreign direct investment in promoting the economic growth of Egypt, is on the period after 1973. The main conclusion is that there has been a significant improvement in the investment climate since 1973 and that foreign investor response and recent and prospective economic trends promise an increasingly fruitful cooperation between Egyptian entities and foreign investors.

To provide perspective to the discussion of developments during the current decade, Chapter 2 is devoted to the three previous growth phases of recent Egyptian economic history. An early growth phase occurred under Mohammed Ali in the first half of the nineteenth century during which an attempt to leapfrog into modern times aborted in the face of foreign hostility. The second growth phase, from about 1920 to the late 1950s, was marked by some frictions and suspicions between foreign and Egyptian businessmen, but this period evidenced greater cooperation and more fruitful joint efforts than the other two periods. There were vigorous governmental efforts to promote new industries and irrigation projects during the succeeding twenty years, but progress was slow in the face of the major suppression of foreign and private enterprise taking place at that time.

As described in Chapter 3, a turn-around in governmental attitudes toward foreign investment has taken place during the 1970s. A legislative breakthrough occurred in 1974 with the promulgation of a comprehensive foreign investment code containing many new positive features. In response to suggestions from foreign investors, the Egyptian government followed through with a 1977 amendment and other regulatory changes, which have vastly improved the legal framework for doing business in Egypt.

The response so far by foreign investors has been rather limited. While a large number of approaches have been made, the actual implementation of projects has fallen far short of initial expectations. Chapter 4 presents the statistical record of foreign projects approved and in operation together with a description of the experience of foreign investors in the banking, petroleum, and other sectors. As I suggest in that chapter, the relatively slow pace of new foreign investment activity is not related to the favorable legal framework but rather to other environmental aspects.

The general economy started to grow at a fast pace during 1975 and may now be on a sustained high-growth path. The open-door policy of the Egyptian government toward foreign and domestic investors and the ensuing revival of private enterprise activity can certainly take some credit for this acceleration in growth. As detailed in Chapter 5, the other significant factors are the reopening of the Suez Canal, the surge in emigrant remittances, the rise in petroleum activity, and substantial foreign assistance. While the expansion in industrial output has not yet been especially vigorous, the underpinnings may have been laid for an incipient breakthrough.

The environmental constraints to strong foreign investor interest in Egypt and to sustained economic growth are discussed in Chapter 6. These constraints are the regional situation of war or peace, relationships with the government, infrastructural facilities, capital and foreign exchange availabilities, and skills. While these constraints have been serious in the past, vigorous steps are now being taken to deal with them. Sufficient progress in removing these constraints has recently been made or is in prospect so that a takeoff to both vigorous foreign investor participation and rapid economic growth may soon take place. A possible outline of future economic growth and some of the likely areas for further foreign business participation are presented in the second section of the concluding chapter.

NOTES

1. Dennis Robertson, "The Future of International Trade," *Economic Journal,* Vol. 48 (March 1938), pp. 4–5.

2. Gottfried Haberler and Robert M. Stern, editors, *Equilibrium and Growth in the World Economy* (Cambridge: Harvard University Press, 1962), p. 242–253, 283–304, 327–335.

3. Charles Issawi, "Egypt Since 1800: A Study in Lopsided Development," *The Journal of Economic History,* Vol. 31 (March 1961), pp. 1–3.

4. Stephen Hymer originated the approach and Richard Caves has probably given the best exposition. See Hymer in Peter Drysdale, ed., *Direct Foreign Investment in Asia and the Pacific* (Toronto: University of Toronto Press, 1972), p. 41; Caves, "International Corporations: The Industrial Economics of Foreign Investment," *Economica,* Vol. 38 (February 1971), pp. 3–6; Harry Johnson in Drysdale, ibid., p. 3; Charles P. Kindleberger, ed., *The International Corporation: A Symposium* (Cambridge: The MIT Press, 1970), pp. 38–39; and W. B. Reddaway, Potter and Taylor, *Effects of U.K. Direct Investment Overseas* (Cambridge: Cambridge University Press, 1968), pp. 308, 335.

5. Some of the best explanations of the efficiency effects of foreign investment include Edith T. Penrose, "Foreign Investment and the Growth of the Firm," *Economic Journal,* Vol. 66 (June 1956), p. 233; A. E. Safarian, "Perspectives on Foreign Direct Investment from the Viewpoint of a Capital Receiving Country." *The Journal of Finance,* Vol. 28 (May 1973), pp. 419–422; Raymond Vernon, *Sovereignty at Bay-The Multinational Spread of U.S. Enterprises* (New York: Basic Books, 1971), pp. 158–162; and Commonwealth of Australia, Treasury Economic Paper No. 1, *Overseas Investment In Australia* (Canberra: Government Printer, May 1972), p. 50.

6. The essential elements of technological know-how are presented in Walter A. Chudson, *The International Transfer of Commercial Technology to Developing Countries,* UNITAR Research Reports No. 13 (United Nations Institute for Training and Research, 1971), pp. 3–5; Jack Baranson, *Industrial Technologies for Developing Economies* (New York: Frederick A. Praeger, 1969), pp. 28–29; and Ingvar Svennilson, "The Transfer of Industrial Know-How to Non-Industrialized Countries," in Kenneth Berrill, ed., *Economic Development with Special Reference to East Asia* (New York: St. Martin's Press, 1964), pp. 407, 412.

7. Accounts of the special advantages accruing to the operations of multinational corporations are contained in Vernon, op. cit., pp. 152–159; United Nations Department of Economic and Social Affairs, *The Impact of Multinational Corporations on Development and on International Relations* (New York: United Nations, 1974), pp. 28, 66; James Brian Quinn, "Technology Transfer by Multinational Companies," *Harvard Business Review,* Vol. 47 (November–Decem-

ber 1969), p. 158; and Raymond F. Mikesell, William H. Bartsch and others, *Foreign Investment in the Petroleum and Mineral Industries* (Baltimore: Johns Hopkins Press, 1971), p. 11.

8. Svennilson, in op. cit., pp. 410–411, states that patents often hide some key element of the production process; if the host country does not possess the necessary complementary know-how, there is no alternative to the direct investment package. F. G. Davidson, in *The Industrialization of Australia* (Melbourne: University of Melbourne, 1957), p. 23, asserts that local firms often find difficulty in employing foreign specialists separately since they prefer the greater job security available in remaining with the large foreign company. See also J. S. Fforde, *An International Trade in Managerial Skills* (Oxford: Basil Blackwell, 1957), pp. 12–14; Jack Baranson, "Transfer of Technical Knowledge by International Corporations to Developing Economies," *American Economic Review,* Vol. 56 (May 1966), p. 276; and Paul Streeten, "Obstacles to Private Foreign Investment in the LDC's," *Columbia Journal of World Business,* Vol. 5 (May–June 1970), p. 32.

9. There are many examples from the Australian experience of the effective transfer of know-how from foreign firms to local affiliates through the provision of detailed designs, formulas, and work methods, through technical help during the "running-in" period, and through frequent training and responsive correction of any technical problems that arise. See Chapter 11 in David W. Carr, *Foreign Investment and Development in the Southwest Pacific: With Special Reference to Australia and Indonesia* (New York: Praeger Special Studies, 1978).

10. Raymond F. Mikesell, ed., *U.S. Private and Government Investment Abroad* (Eugene: University of Oregon Press, 1962), pp. 122, 138. See also Svennilson, ibid., pp. 407–426; United Nations, op. cit., pp. 33–35, 72; Fforde, op. cit., pp. 21, 97; Baranson, ibid., pp. 259–261 and in "Technology Transfer Through the International Firm," *American Economic Review,* Vol. 60 (May 1970), pp. 435–437; Quinn, op. cit., p. 150; and John J. Dunning, "Technology, United States Investment and European Economic Growth" in Kindleberger, op. cit., pp. 170–172.

PREVIOUS GROWTH PHASES

A significant feature of Egypt's three previous growth phases was the discordance between foreign participation in the Egyptian economy and domestic entrepreneurial activity. Whenever foreign involvement was significant, Egyptians were lethargic, and when Egyptians were creative or energetic, foreign interests were hostile or not very actively involved. There was either a fundamental lack of strong cooperation between foreign and Egyptian entities or a catalytic role on the part of foreign interests. Foreign firms did not act as an engine of growth in stimulating creative responses by Egyptians in diverse sectors.

An early growth phase occurred under Mohammed Ali (1816–49) during whose rule an attempt was made to modernize the country in the face of foreign hostility. Following that failure, the transition to an export-oriented economy was swift. The second growth phase ran from about 1920 to the late 1950s and was marked by an emergence of national enterprise. While there were some frictions and suspicions between foreign and Egyptian businessmen, this period did evidence greater cooperation and fruitful joint efforts than the other two periods. The third growth phase lasted until the early 1970s, and, in the context of "Arab socialism" and political turmoil, a major suppression of foreign and Egyptian private enterprise took place. In spite of vigorous governmental efforts to promote new industries and general development, the pace of progress was slow in the face of isolation from foreign business creativity and of the constraints on Egyptian entrepreneurs.

MOHAMMED ALI'S DEFIANCE OF THE WEST

Mohammed Ali was remarkably successful in his efforts to establish a diverse range of fairly modern industries. After his death, however, the indus-

11

tries collapsed and the diversification of the economy was blocked due to foreign intervention and the absence of an Egyptian entrepreneurial and professional class.

Early Success

Mohammed Ali's dream was grandiose in that he attempted to move directly from a subsistence economy to a modern industrialized one in two or three short decades. Six major aspects of that revolution were as follows: 1) the prevailing system of communal ownership was replaced by individual ownership, large tracts of land being given to relatives or followers of Ali; 2) major irrigation works were undertaken to replace basin irrigation with perennial irrigation and to expand the cultivated area from 3.1 million acres in 1813 to 4.2 million acres by 1852; 3) the planting of long-staple cotton was started on a commercial scale in 1821, and by 1845, seventeen million pounds per year of cotton were being exported; 4) communications were developed mainly in order to facilitate foreign trade, one example being the improvement of the port of Alexandria and the canal linking it to the Nile; 5) Ali monopolized trade by buying crops from farmers at low fixed prices and selling them to foreign exporters at great profits. He also directly imported about two-fifths of the goods brought into Egypt; and 6) the principal aspect of Ali's revolution was his attempt to establish a modern and diversified industry entirely owned and controlled by the state.[1]

The range of factories established between 1816 and 1836 in many parts of Egypt is impressive. The weaving of cotton textiles was the major industry but also introduced were cotton ginning, and rice milling, and industries producing sugar and rum, edible oils, dairy products, indigo, linen, woolen fabrics, silk, ropes, leather, glass, books, paper, saltpeter, and sulfuric acid. Military arsenals put out swords, rifles, cannon, and gun powder, while iron foundries fabricated many of the tools and simple machine parts used in the textile plants.

Visitors to Egypt at the time commented that Egyptian workers became dexterous in using modern equipment and that the general work efficiency and techniques at the foundries and arsenals were nearly as good as in France. The iron castings were of high quality and not more than one quarter more expensive than abroad. Egyptian indigo and cotton yarn were fully competitive with foreign production and were even exported, but most other Egyptian products were more expensive.[2]

The total investments in industrial establishments may have amounted to 12 million and were obtained from trade monopoly profits, taxation, and forced loans. Some 70,000 workers were employed at the peak. The necessary unskilled labor was conscripted and paid low wages, while foreign technicians, managers, and skilled workers were well paid. A market for the output of the factories was provided by the expanding armed forces, by import substitution, and by displacing some handicrafts.

Much of the success of the new plants was due to the hiring of foreign managers and technicians and to the vigorous training programs. Foreign managers and technicians were particularly numerous in the arsenals, foundries, and cotton textile plants. The foreigners afforded crucial assistance in installing new equipment, imitating the simpler imported parts for local reproduction, and in upgrading Egyptian techniques. Numerous Egyptians were trained in the new skills: over 300 were sent to Europe and a thousand or so studied in the newly opened schools of medicine, engineering, chemistry, and accounting, as well as in the military and naval colleges.[3]

The Failure of the Ali Revolution

Ali's program of forced industrialization enjoyed significant early success thanks primarily to the administrative protection that he accorded his infant industries. These industries, however, did not long outlive that protection. The collapse of Ali's industries was followed by the integration of Egypt, as an agricultural unit, in the worldwide economic system.

Much of the reason for the failure of Ali's revolution can be attributed to foreign interference. Britain and France did not welcome the threatened emergence of Egypt as an independent economic and military power. European economic thinkers and businessmen, espousing the theory of comparative advantage and free trade, felt that agricultural countries should content themselves with agricultural output to assure an international economic balance; they therefore opposed Ali's system of state monopoly and protective measures for Egyptian industry. In 1820, European pressure temporarily secured a low 3 percent duty on all Egyptian imports; this was supplanted by an 1838 Anglo-Ottoman treaty for a higher 12 percent rate provided that Ali abandon his state monopolies. Ali, however, ignored the treaty and continued his monopolies. After an Egyptian military defeat by the British and French, the 1841 treaty cut back the permissible Egyptian military forces, reduced the general import duty to 5 percent, and finally abolished the monopolies while securing the entry of foreign traders into Egypt. Ali's encouragement and protection of Egyptian industry waned, and the exposure to the competition of European industry increased. His factories declined and, except for the government printing press, did not survive his death in 1849.

The other reasons for the failure of Ali's revolution were the backwardness of the country and the very authoritarianism which facilitated the early successes. A middle class did not exist, and one was not created during Ali's tenure to carry on significant commercial activities outside the state monopolies or to continue industrial ventures when the state ones collapsed. The government monopoly of commerce and the tight state control over general economic life led to a decline in the number of Egyptian merchants and private artisans and prevented the emergence of Egyptian private entrepreneurs.[4]

Industrial development and economic diversification languished during the period 1850–1920 which was characterized by a free trade regime[5] and the nonemergence of Egyptian capitalists. Egypt developed as a one-crop agricultural economy where nearly all activities were geared to the cultivation and export of cotton. Success in the cotton sector is indicated by the rise of cotton exports from 17 million pounds in 1845 to 250 million in 1920. The large-scale immigration of foreigners[6] and the $400 million or so invested in Egypt by foreigners until 1914 were largely connected with the expansion of cotton production or to related financing, transport, and trading activities. The influx of foreign capital and personnel failed to stimulate the development of economic sectors outside cotton or to promote the emergence of Egyptian entrepreneurs and professionals.

The single major development unrelated to cotton was the opening of the Suez Canal in 1869. Although the canal permitted a large flow of international traffic through Egypt, the early gains to Egypt were small. The local expenditures of the Suez Canal Company and the annual payment to the Egyptian government did not exceed $10 million per year even by 1940 and $35 million by 1955.[7]

The only industries established by 1910 were those related to the elementary processing of the export crop and those protected by natural advantages, such as a few textile and cement plants, cotton gins, bakeries, and companies making soap, sugar, and beer. These few industries were almost exclusively financed and owned by foreign companies or foreign residents.

Several attempts to establish industrial plants failed and resulted in large losses. Two Egyptian landowners established a glass factory in Alexandria in 1885, but the plant soon closed down in the face of foreign competition. Another Egyptian group founded a textile plant in 1896, which was then sold to British investors. The British colonial government, in zealous adherence to free-trade theory, decided in 1901 that it was unfair that the textile plant enjoy the benefit of the general import duty of 8 percent. The government imposed an excise duty on domestic production equal to that on imports and the plant collapsed in 1907.[8]

Development during this whole period was thus of a lopsided or enclave type with few benefits accruing to the economy at large and Egyptian creativity apparently being stifled. The cotton export surplus was in fact absorbed in the servicing of a huge foreign debt incurred as a result of extravagant life styles and other budgetary excesses; little of it was reinvested in other sectors. Foreign residents or minority groups not only controlled finance and large-scale commerce but even dominated petty trade, such as shoe repair and tailoring. Practically all physicians, engineers, and other professionals were non-Egyptian. It was not until the 1920s and 1930s that an Egyptian business and professional class began to emerge.

Various reasons have been cited for the long stagnation in Egyptian business activities. A partial explanation is that under the Capitulations agreed to in the 1841 treaty and lasting until 1937, foreigners enjoyed fiscal and judicial immunity, and their financial and commercial links with European markets gave them further advantages over Egyptian competitors. The opportunities for enormous speculative gains in cotton and land may have absorbed much of the creative energies and savings of Egyptians, with land prices frequently soaring to phenomenal heights. The basic reason for the stagnation was the laissez-faire policy of the British colonial government, which favored strict specialization in the production and export of cotton and discouraged other activities.[9] In nearly every country, the beginnings of industrialization and the development of indigenous enterprise apparently require temporary governmental protection and promotion, and this lack in Egypt, combined with the low creativity and entrepreneurial spirit among private Egyptians, until about 1920, prevented the diffusion of gains from foreign activity.

THE EMERGENCE OF PRIVATE EGYPTIAN ENTERPRISE

The emergence of Egyptian enterprise began to take place during the 1920s and 1930s as a result of World War I and economic instability and the general fall in cotton export prices. Industrial expansion was furthered with increasingly strong government support. The establishment of new industries and the participation of increasing numbers of Egyptian entrepreneurs and skilled workers were facilitated through the 1950s by fairly numerous instances of cooperation between foreign and domestic businesses.

World War I and Cotton Export Instability as Major Causes of the Emergence of National Enterprises

The effects of World War I stimulated the emergence of Egytian enterprise in two major ways. Trade had been cut off so that artificial protection had to be afforded during much of the war to many emerging industries. By 1916, additional plants were created for furniture, pottery, processed foods, rugs, simple agricultural and industrial machinery, and some leather, copper, and metal products.

Secondly, World War I led to much higher prices and monopoly profits for the several large-scale commercial and industrial ventures that were largely in foreign hands. These high prices and profits were attacked in the

Egyptian press, with the foreign-controlled Egyptian Salt and Soda Company and the Egyptian Sugar Company receiving special attention. Press statements expressed the belief that the situation would be cured if Egyptians financed and operated the firms and they accordingly urged action in this direction. The Egyptian revolution of 1919 in the political sphere, with the emergence of the Wafd political party, had its counterpart in the economic sphere, with much jealousy engendered at the overweening economic power of foreigners and with a determination to strike down the colonial economic system and strive for economic independence and diversification.[10]

Successive declines in the price of cotton in 1920, 1921, and 1926, which culminated in the Depression of 1929–32, and the marked deterioration in Egypt's terms of trade during the 1930s and 1940s brought home to many Egyptian landowners and merchants the dangers of reliance on a one-crop economy and the consequent need to diversify. The sharp price swings had caused large losses for some Egyptians, while the long-term trend of declining profits in cotton production and marketing also acted to encourage investments outside agriculture.

The Beginnings of Strong Government Support

The expiration of a trade convention with Italy in February 1930 helped to restore fiscal autonomy to Egypt. A comprehensive tariff schedule was issued the same month, replacing the previous general import duty of 8 percent with a new 4 percent rate for raw materials, 6–10 percent for industrial equipment and components, 15 percent for most finished manufactured goods, and 20–30 percent for certain luxury goods, such as alcoholic beverages, cigarettes, and perfumes. The 8 percent excise tax on textile manufactures was abolished. Several increases in tariffs took place during the 1930s and 1940s, especially on textiles, footwear, and sugar. For example, the rate on cotton yarn was 30 percent in 1949. During the 1950s, tariffs and special duties were increased across the board on several occasions so that the effective rate of protection on most manufactured goods came to exceed 30 percent, with many effective rates above 58 percent, and the average duty payable around 100 percent.[11]

Other policies indicating government encouragement to industry included preferential railway rates and a 10 percent price preference for Egyptians on governmental purchases of some products during the 1920s; this preference was applied to all products after July 1930. Tax incentives and export subsidies were also increasingly granted, while in 1949 the government supplied 51 percent of the funds for the establishment of an Industrial Bank. The bank had a slow start, however, with annual loan rates rising only to £E2 million in 1958 and to £E4.2 million in 1960. The leading recipients were the engineering and mechanical, textile, and building materials industries. During World War II, an elaborate system of direct import controls was set up and not fully dismantled after the war. With increasing foreign exchange shortages in the 1950s import quotas and licensing came to be applied ever more rigorously. Direct import controls came to outweigh high tariffs as a protective device to promote the establishment and expansion of Egyptian industry.

Some Cooperation between Foreign and Domestic Business

I noted earlier that one of the reasons for the emergence of Egyptian enterprise after World War I was the criticism of allegedly rapacious foreign profits. On the other hand, there were close contacts between many members of the resident foreign business community and emerging Egyptian entrepreneurs for the purpose of removing obstructions to the establishment of local industry and of opening some specific industrial plants. Later, there was also some cooperation between overseas and Egyptian investors. Increasing participation by Egyptians in the new plants and a little industrial diversification had taken place by the 1950s.

Formation of Egyptian Institutions to Promote Industrialization

The end of World War I had led to a breakdown of the artificial protection that some emerging industries temporarily enjoyed. There was, therefore, a desire to create a pressure group to restore some protection from imports and to work for the adoption of other governmental policies favorable to the development of Egyptian industry. The Federation of Industries was accordingly established in June 1922. The sharp fall in cotton prices during 1920–21 stimulated the birth of the Egyptian General Agriculture Syndicate, whose objective was to wrest from foreign control the financing and marketing of cotton. Specifically Egyptian-owned financial institutions were lacking in the financial sphere. Bank Misr was founded on March 8, 1920, to fill this gap, "to encourage various enterprises and to assist in the establishment of financial, commercial, industrial, agricultural, transportation and insurance companies."[12]

The Federation of Industries was largely pioneered by the newly confident and resurgent foreign business community resident in Egypt; yet it struggled against overseas commercial interests and colonial government attitudes, especially the theories of laissez-faire and free trade cotton specialization, which the Federation believed were obstructing the development of Egyptian industry. The original members of the industrial chambers making up the Federation represented such products as sugar, building materials, salt, cotton yarn, clothing, and mining. In time, an increasing percentage of new Federation members was Egyptian-born. In 1925, Egyptians represented 22 percent of Federation membership. This was also the year that Bank Misr and its associated Egyptian industrial firms joined the Federation. The percentage of Egyptian members rose to 27 by 1939. The percentage rise for new members was much sharper: from 12 percent for the period 1925–30, 20 percent for 1930–36, and 52 percent for 1936–39.[13]

The basic goal of Bank Misr was to mobilize Egyptian capital and to create Egyptian-run industries and other organs to diversify economic activities and give Egyptians more influence in their own economy. The Bank felt that there was plenty of idle Egyptian capital in land, in foreign banks, or just being hoarded. The bank's original capital was £E80,000 and rose to £E1 million by 1927, pledged by landowners and a few big merchants. A major activity was investment in the shipping of agricultural products and granting loans to agricultural cooperatives in order to get better prices for Egyptian farmers and to lessen foreign control over agricultural marketing.

In 1923, Bank Misr began to use some of its profits to assist in the establishment of small-scale industries. Nine companies were formed before 1930, in the fields of paper, cotton ginning, silk weaving, fish, and flax. The biggest venture was Misr Cotton Spinning & Weaving Company, which absorbed two-thirds of the capital of the Misr group companies founded during the 1920s, or £E300,000.[14] The foreign commercial banks also occasionally participated in the creation of new enterprises and frequently made short-term advances to local industry, but their activities in the industrial sphere were much less significant than those of Misr.

Involvement of Overseas Capital

The announcement of the comprehensive tariff schedule of 1930 quickened the pace of Egyptian industrialization and, as it happened, the trend of Bank Misr's policies to promote industrialization changed about the same time. Bank Misr had hired foreign experts in such areas as accounting and cotton shipping, but before 1930 it had eschewed cooperation with foreign equity capital. In 1929, the Bank felt that the Egyptian capital it had succeeded in mobilizing already or expected to mobilize would be insufficient to bring about rapid industrialization despite the customs protection promised for the following year. In a report to the Egyptian government, the Bank, therefore, urged the creation of a government-supported industrial bank.[15] The failure of the Egyptian government to accept this suggestion at that time made Bank Misr resolve to cooperate with overseas investors to obtain the needed capital for a faster rate of industrialization. Twelve enterprises were formed through the good offices of Bank Misr during the 1930s; additional fields covered were drugs and building materials. A significant feature of the largest enterprises was the entry of overseas capital. Examples were Misr Air Works Company with 40 percent British capital, a spinning and dyeing company with 50 percent British capital, an insurance company with British and Italian equity participation, and shipping and tourism companies with some British participation.[16] The overall significance of Bank Misr's efforts to promote industrialization in Egypt can be visualized by the fact that the shares of Bank Misr industrial companies established between 1922 and 1938 amounted to £E2.5 million, or 45 percent of the increase in the total paid-up capital of all joint stock industrial companies during that period.[17]

Increasing Participation of Egyptian Personnel

Egyptians became increasingly involved in industrial companies. In 1931, 50 of 504 directors of joint stock companies were Egyptian, and, in 1937, 72 of 496 directors were Egyptians. By 1951, the percentage of Egyptian directors had risen to 35. Many of the early Egyptian directors were not really businessmen but ex-civil servants, politicans, professionals, or others who might have been included as part of an Egyptianization program for publicity purposes, rather than based on intrinsic merits.[18] Later, more of the appointed Egyptians were businessmen.

During World War II, the British military provided extensive training in diverse skills to 200,000 workers. During the 1940s and 1950s there was an expansion of technical and general education and of company in-service training programs. Thousands of Egyptians also returned from overseas training courses. Additional upgrading of local skills was provided through the visits of foreign technicians when installing new equipment. Thus, the new industrial plants were well supplied with Egyptian technicians.[19]

In contrast to the almost total absence of Egyptian professionals almost until the 1920s, there has been a large increase during the 1930s, 1940s, and 1950s. The number of physicians rose from 3,300 in 1937 to 5,700 in 1947 and to about 10,000 in 1960, and that of teachers from 35,000 to 52,000 and 111,000. The 1947 census listed 16,000 engineers, 5,000 lawyers, and 1,600 chemists and pharmacists.[20]

The large size of the foreign population in Egypt induced the Egyptian government to promote the employment of more Egyptians, especially in view of the tendency of foreign companies to employ members of their own minority groups. According to the 1917 census, the foreign population in Egypt numbered 202,000, comprising 24,000 British, 21,000 French, 40,000 Italians, 57,000 Greeks, and 60,000 Jews. In 1937, foreigners numbered about 240,000 and then declined to 204,000 in 1947, and t0 143,000 in 1960.[21] Presure to increase the percentage of Egyptians employed in business, was formalized in the 1947 joint stock companies laws. At least 51 percent of a company's capital and 40 percent of its Board of Directors must be Egyptian. Seventy-five percent of the employees receiving 65 percent of the total salaries, and 90 percent of the laborers receiving 80 percent of the wages paid, must also be Egyptian. Any temporary exception was carefully reviewed by the Ministry of Commerce and Industry.[22]

The operation of the Suez Canal came to involve an increasing number of Egyptians. Thousands of Egyptian workers were, of course, involved in the initial building of the canal and in the seven programs of improvement executed between 1876 and 1954. The bulk of the workers performing maintenance tasks and conducting the simpler aspects of operations have also been Egyptians. On the other hand, the responsible positions have long been occupied by Europeans. Since the 1930s the Egyptian government has been annoyed at this situation and has pressured for the inclusion of more Egyptians. Such pressure was increasingly effective, but, even as late as 1946, only 2 of the 28 members of the Board of Directors were Egyptians, and most of the pilots, technicians, and administrative personnel were foreigners. The Egyptian government secured a new agreement for increasing Egyptianization in March 1949 so that by July 1956, 40 of the 205 pilots were Egyptians as were 413 of the 805 other administrative and technical personnel.[23] To give the reader an idea of the rapid expansion in the scope of the activities of the Suez Canal, Table 2.1 presents the numbers and tonnage of the transiting ships during the 1870–1966 period.

Statistics on company ownership and on investment funds show a similar pattern of increasing Egyptian participation and, especially after World War II, decreasing foreign investor participation. In 1914, 8 percent of the capital in joint stock companies was controlled by Egyptians, and even by 1933 only 9 percent of the total capital was owned by Egyptians. This ownership share

TABLE 2.1: Numbers and Tonnages of Ships Passing through the Suez Canal, 1870–1966

Year	Total Number of Transits	Net Suez Tonnage
1870	486	436,609
1880	2,026	3,057,422
1890	3,389	6,890,094
1900	3,441	9,738,152
1910	4,533	16,581,898
1920	4,009	17,574,657
1930	5,761	31,668,759
1940	2,589	13,535,712
1950	11,751	81,795,523
1955	14,666	115,756,398
1960	18,734	185,322,000
1965	20,289	246,817,000
1966	21,250	274,250,000

Source: Suez Canel Authority, *Annual Report* for various years.

rose gradually to perhaps 50 percent by 1956. For companies newly established during 1934–39, the Egyptian ownership share was 47 percent, for those established during 1940–45 it was 66 percent, and during 1946–48 it was 84 percent.[24] In 1956, the Census of Industrial Production for that year showed that of 3,514 enterprises employing ten persons or more, only 632 belonged to foreigners and 84 were of mixed nationality.[25]

Aside from the £E84 million invested in the Suez Canal, the value of foreign investments in 1933 was £E81 million. French investments, mainly in mortgage banking and public utilities, accounted for £E39 million. British investments were mostly in industrial firms and mortgage banks, accounting for £E32 million. Belgian investments of £7 million were mostly in land companies.[26] While foreign investment activity remained prominent through 1952, or so, there was a sharp drop in new investments afterwards. New British investments went mainly into engineering and chemicals and American investments into petroleum, tires, and chemicals. Additional investments were made by Belgians, Swiss, Germans, Lebanese, Kuwaitis, and Saudis. Direct investments from overseas between 1952 and 1961 totaled only £E9 million, of which £E5.2 million went into petroleum.

Some Economic Diversification Achieved

Since the development of cotton was the focus of economic activity in the 1850–1920 period, we will now take a brief look at the status of cotton. The statistics on cotton production and acreage given in Table 2.2 reveal

TABLE 2.2: Cotton Production and Acreage, 1915–76

Period	Area (thousands of feddans)	Production (thousands of tons)
Average, 1915–19	1,482	238
Average, 1920–24	1,684	278
Average, 1925–29	1,761	344
Average, 1930–34	1,679	321
Average, 1935–39	1,754	411
Average, 1940–44	1,120	270
Average, 1945–49	1,316	317
Average, 1950–54	1,765	372
Average, 1955–59	1,791	394
Average, 1960–64	1,751	444
Average, 1965–69	1,692	470
Average, 1970–76	1,517	450

Sources: Until 1964, Donald C. Mead, *Growth and Structural Change in the Egyptian Economy* (Homewood, Illinois: Richard D. Irwin, 1967), p. 322; thereafter, National Bank of Egypt, *Economic Bulletin* (No. 3, 1977), Table 4/2 A.

progress very much slower than that attained before 1920. Whereas cotton exports had expanded fifteen-fold from 1845 to 1920, continued massive investments in irrigation and fertilizers only succeeded in raising cotton production by about 33 percent between the early 1920s and early 1950s and by about 25 percent more until the early 1970s.

The existence of some cooperation between foreign and domestic business and the emergence of Egyptian enterpreneurs did succeed in promoting the expansion in output of some simple consumer products and in achieving a small amount of industrial diversification by the 1950s. Statistics on the output of several products is given in Table 2.3. Products showing the highest rates of increase in output from 1920 to 1950 are cotton textiles and cement. Significant expansion also took place in the production of glass, leather, and preserved foods.

Industrial diversification has taken place primarily in the range of consumer nondurables. The development was of an import-substitution type with less than 10 percent of the total manufacturing output exported. By the end of the 1930s, output became significant in sugar, alcohol, cigarettes, salt, flour, cotton yarns, shoes, cement, soap, beer, vegetable oil, paper, matches, and metallic furniture.[27] World War II caused a further quickening of the industrial pace as a result of a surge in wealth, a sharp drop in imports, and, as already noted, significant training experiences. The industries introduced in the early postwar period and in the 1950s included chemicals, pharmaceuticals, kitchen utensils, stoves, super-phosphates, tires, processed foods, batteries, refrigerators, beverages, bulbs, radios, cables and tubes, diesel engines, bicycles, sewing machines, tractors, railway cars, and auto-

TABLE 2.3: Production of Several Industrial Commodities, 1920–50

Commodity	Unit	1920*	1930	1940	1950
Cotton yarn and thread	thousands of tons	1	3	25	52
Mechanically woven cotton cloth	m. sq. yds.	9	20	159	—
Refined sugar	thousands of tons	79	109	224	287
Milled rice	thousands of tons	—	244	470	842
Beer	m. liters	—	7	16	13
Soap	thousands of tons	—	38	45	65
Cement	thousands of tons	24	190	370	994
Petroleum	thousands of tons	—	287	938	2,324
Crude phosphates	thousands of tons	—	313	281	449

*Where possible, the figure quoted is a three-year average. If not, the nearest total to the above years has been selected.

Source: Patrick O'Brien, The Revolution in Egypt's Economic System (New York: Oxford University Press, 1966), p. 15.

mobiles.[28] The total employment in industrial plants with ten or more employees had risen in tandem with the fairly sizable industrial expansion and diversification from 35,000 in 1916 to 95,000 in 1927, and to 265,000 in 1954.[29]

GOVERNMENT DOMINATION OF MAJOR ECONOMIC ACTIVITIES

The fifteen years between about 1956 and 1971 witnessed a sharp increase in the role of the government in the economic life of Egypt. Foreign investors were almost completely squeezed out. During the latter part of the period, there was apparently a decline in the efficiency and competitiveness of much of Egyptian industry and a slowdown in overall economic progress.

The Drastic Decline in the Role of Foreign Business and the Private Sector

The members of the Revolutionary Council which overthrew King Farouk in 1952 did not then have any definite economic ideology, other than unhappiness about the privileged position of the wealthy landed elite. President Nasser and other leaders stated in the early 1950s that the policy of the government was to eliminate the special privileges of the wealthy, but otherwise to encourage the private sector in every way possible.[30] The comprehensive agrarian reform measures of 1952 and 1961 were primarily designed to achieve the former objective by setting maximum limits on individual land ownership and expropriating the remainder. As for the latter objective, several changes were made in the tariffs; the duties were raised on competing manufactured goods and abolished or reduced on raw materials and equipment. Law No. 430 was passed in 1953 to exempt newly approved companies from income tax for seven years, and plant expansions were exempted from tax for five years. A more liberal attitude was also exhibited toward foreign capital in four laws approved in 1953 and 1954. Under these laws, foreign investors were allowed to have majority control of companies operating in Egypt, rather than only 49 percent according to the 1947 law, and provisions regarding the transfer of profits and original capital abroad were also eased. The Mining and Quarrying Law of 1953 was considerably more liberal than that of 1948 in that it permitted the granting of new concessions to foreign as well as domestic petroleum companies and allowed longer extensions.[31]

Egypt's international relations worsened during 1955 and 1956, the low point being the abrupt withdrawal of an American/British/World Bank offer to finance the Aswan High Dam project. President Nasser countered on July

20, 1956, by nationalizing the Suez Canal. This event marks a watershed in the policy of the Egyptian government toward foreign business and indeed toward private enterprise in general.

Aside from the six-month interval of hostilities in October and November 1956 and the clearance operations afterwards, the nationalization of the canal was achieved with little disruption, and the results were highly beneficial for Egypt. The number of Egyptian pilots rose from 40 in 1956 to 129 in 1960 out of a total of 216 in that year, and the number of technicians and administrative personnel rose from 413 to 858 out of 900 in 1960.[32] Egyptian government revenues from the canal's operations, with the full toll receipts remaining in Egypt, immediately rose to £E30 million, and by 1966 to £E95 million.

The nationalization of the Suez Canal and the outbreak of war in the fall of 1956 led Egypt to take hostile actions against foreign businesses and set the stage for increasing governmental curbs on the Egyptian private sector as well. In October 1956, Egypt sequestered the property belonging to all British and French subjects and to many Jewish subjects and nationalized all British and French companies. In reaction to the events in the Congo in December 1960, Belgian interests were nationalized as well. A law was passed in 1957 requiring that all financial institutions not already nationalized be Egyptianized* within five years, with all shares to be owned by Egyptians and all members of the Boards of Directors and managers to be Egyptian. Other laws during 1957 required insurance companies to follow suit and stipulated that executives of export and import agencies and commercial representatives should be Egyptian citizens within five years. A law was passed in August 1958 reversing the favorable 1953 law and again providing, as in the 1947 law, that a majority of Boards of Directors be Egyptian.[33] By 1960 as a result of all these laws, the percentage of European company directors fell to 8 percent from 30 percent in 1951. Of 1,007 names listed in 1961 as owners of shares of over £E10,000 or more in 148 large companies, only 4 percent were European.[34]

As part of the general nationalization measures in July 1961, most of the remaining foreign investments were taken over by the government. Other than joint venture agreements with the government concluded by three foreign drug companies in the early 1960s and continuing investments by foreign petroleum companies, foreign investment in Egypt was negligible in the period from 1956 to 1971.

Concomitant with the near elimination of the foreign investor presence in Egypt has been the increasing economic role of the Egyptian government and the drastic decline in the role of the private sector. Until 1953, participa-

---

*Nationalization means the transfer from private to public management or control, while Egyptianization means the transfer from foreign to Egyptian management or control.

tion by the government in industry was minimal, consisting of a petroleum refinery, some printing presses, and repair shops for railways, cars, and ships. During "the free enterprise" phase of the revolution, lasting until 1956, the government participated together with private capital in a few large industrial schemes, such as iron and steel works, fertilizers, and railway equipment, and it nationalized a few public utilities. Government participation also took place during 1956 and early 1957 in companies for mineral and petroleum exploitation, marine transport, and petroleum trade.

The years 1956–61 witnessed a growing participation of the government in the economic life of the country, both through government acquisitions and through government regulations and controls. The wave of comprehensive nationalizations was foreshadowed in February 1960, when disagreement arose with the Bank Misr group over the direction of private investment, the result being the group's nationalization. The laws of July 1961 decreed a sweeping nationalization of the private sector, including the leading navigation company, cotton-pressing establishments, the gas and electricity company of Alexandria, the Cairo Tramway Company, all banks and insurance companies, and 42 large industrial, transport, commercial, financial, and land reclamation companies. Fifty percent of all cotton exporting firms were nationalized, as were 82 other companies. The stock exchanges and the cotton futures market were closed down, and individuals and corporations were prohibited from owning more than £E10,000 in shares in each of 148 major companies. Imports could only be made through government-owned companies, and commercial agencies must be at least 25 percent government-owned. All public works on behalf of government departments and agencies, valued at £E30,000 or over, must be undertaken by companies with at least 50 percent government equity participation. During the domestic political turmoil following the breakaway of Syria from the union with Egypt in September 1961, the government launched a vigorous press campaign against "reactionary, feudalist and capitalist elements," and the property of 850 persons was sequestrated.[35]

The result of all these acts of nationalization was that the share of the government sector in the national income may have risen from less than 20 percent in 1959 to 40 percent in 1963 and 50 percent by 1967. By 1967, the Egyptian government share in industrial value added was 64 percent, and in firms with ten or more employees it was 90 percent. Private enterprise remained significant only in retail trade, handicrafts and repair services, housing, the service sector, agriculture, and in the smaller, less modern, industrial plants.[36]

Extensive government intervention increased in scope vis-à-vis the firms remaining in private hands. The Ministry of Industry was formed in 1957 and was given increasing authority over pricing and output decisions, over the allocations of capital goods and raw materials, as well as over employment and wages. All investment planning and decisions emanated from the government, and any firm planning to expand or to restrict output required the specific approval of the government. Three laws issued in July 1961 decreed that 25 percent of the profits of all companies be allocated to its employees, prohibited any company director or employee from earning more than £E5,000 per annum, and decreed that all Boards of Directors must include two employees or workers among its seven members. Import and foreign exchange controls remained rigorous. In this context of government encroachment and control, there was little room left for private initiative or profit incentive, and Egypt's entrepreneurial spirit appeared to have languished.

Declining Efficiency and Competitiveness of Much of Egyptian Industry

While the growth of exports of manufactured goods had been fairly substantial throughout the 1950s and 1960s, other indicators of efficiency showed a declining trend after 1962. Many sectors of Egyptian industry became less competitive, and a part of the explanation appears to lie in the isolation from foreign contacts and the suppression of private initiative.

A picture of the trends in the exports of manufactured goods from 1946 to 1970 can be obtained from Table 2.4. Except for the periods 1951–55 and 1965–68, such exports expanded fairly substantially throughout the two-and-a-half decades, and generally constituted approximately 9 percent of total industrial output. Since the early 1950s, textiles have accounted for 55–66 percent of manufactured goods exports, with footwear, furniture, chemicals, and machinery growing in importance. Manufactured goods other than textiles and petroleum products grew by a respectable average annual rate of 13.7 percent from 1952/53 to 1969/70.[37]

A few industries remained competitive throughout the period by means of high or increasing productivity. Such industries included those producing sugar, cement, fertilizer, tires, drugs, and cosmetics, and perhaps textiles. These industries remained competitive primarily because local materials make up a high proportion of the total value added. Thus, for example, cement plants were built near abundant raw materials, a super phosphate factory utilized good local phosphate rock, and packaging represents a high percentage of value added in the drug and cosmetics industry and can be done cheaply in Egypt. It is also probable that improving technology was a factor in the rising productivity in regard to nitrate fertilizers, tires, and cement. Competitiveness in textile production has been reduced by the almost continuous enforcement since 1916 of a governmental ban on imports of cheap short staple cotton; the Egyptian long staple variety is considerably more expensive. Textile production costs are also influenced by the high tariffs on cloth imports.[38]

TABLE 2.4: Value of Manufacturing Exports, 1946–70 (£E000s)

	1946	1949	1951	1953	1955	1958	1961	1963	1965	1966	1968	1970
Food	2,232	1,876	2,494	2,158	2,149	2,317	5,110	4,501	4,593	6,202	5,211	6,286
Beverages	11	9	8	129	42	170	181	240	218	362	2,569	2,556
Tobacco	351	50	99	121	70	95	103	223	660	836	608	340
Cotton yarn	39	1,869	6,962	2,566	4,383	7,083	7,727	18,187	31,092	30,879	29,922	35,629
Cotton fabrics	8	317	620	497	999	4,586	6,139	9,006	11,677	13,476	14,521	18,132
Other textiles, waste	432	310	1,018	936	933	2,346	1,827	3,222	1,821	2,159	4,376	6,380
Clothing, footwear	339	228	258	327	501	759	694	543	1,020	1,266	5,756	8,061
Leather, rubber	314	240	243	221	411	644	698	1,066	325	400	612	1,284
Books and printed matter	123	89	355	435	658	938	1,069	1,561	3,029	1,825	1,869	1,958
Petroleum products	1,533	2,594	2,282	951	1,020	2,283	1,610	6,296	10,175	9,213	1,539	485
Chemicals	426	370	810	2,364	970	911	665	1,583	1,878	2,002	3,212	9,228
Nonmetal products	131	39	119	658	260	1,271	3,270	1,882	2,284	2,594	5,403	2,176
Metals and metal products	579	90	78	168	361	335	945	571	506	413	883	840
Machinery and transport equipment	8	37	102	13	23	60	145	271	1,261	2,064	1,873	1,699
Miscellaneous	189	2,924	35	732	836	768	524	1,496	5,047	5,015	1,445	9,608
Total £E000s	6,705	11,042	15,483	12,276	13,616	24,566	30,707	50,648	75,586	78,706	79,799	104,662

Source: Robert Mabro and Samir Radwan, *The Industrialization of Egypt, 1939–73—Policy and Performance* (New York: Oxford University Press, 1976), p. 220.

For most industries, the productivity trend was adverse. Mabro and Radwan have made some detailed calculations as to total factor productivity and output per man-hour from 1939 to 1969/70, as shown in Table 2.5.[39] Output per man-hour is calculated to have increased by a fairly impressive 4 or 5 percent per year on the average from 1939 to 1962, but then to have collapsed by 5.5 percent annually from 1963/64 to 1969/70. The growth in total factor productivity was highest during World War II, became relatively modest from 1945 to 1962, and collapsed afterwards.

TABLE 2.5: Growth of Industrial Output and of Total Factor Productivity, 1939–70 (average annual percent rates)

	1939–45	1945–54	1954–62	1963/64– 1969/70
Output	5.14	7.72	9.67	2.00
Labor inputs	1.49	2.72	4.57	8.02
Capital inputs	−4.00	8.62	8.16	0.54
TFP	6.70	1.37	2.88	−1.90
Output per man-hour	3.6	5.2	4.4	−5.5

Source: Mabro and Radwan, op. cit., pp. 147, 183.

The causes of the fall in productivity and declining competitiveness among the bulk of Egyptian industries after 1963 lay in shortages of capital and foreign exchange, misallocation of investment resources, and badly applied wage and employment policies. Many of these defects, largely of government policy, would have been less serious if there had been foreign investor participation or more leeway for decision making by private management. After all, foreign investors could have filled part of the capital and foreign exchange gaps, through the resources they can supply directly and through their ability to stimulate host resources into more fruitful activity. If private managers had not been so hamstrung by governmental regulations, the misallocation of resources would probably have been less acute and the cost escalation through bad wage and employment policies would have been less serious.

The shortage of investment capital has been a major long-standing weakness of Egyptian economic development. Gross fixed capital formation as a percentage of the gross domestic product had risen to the ten to fifteen percent area as early as the 1880s but has not consistently risen above that area since. The savings ratio fell during the interwar period and then rose sharply to over 25 percent during World War II, before falling back to about 13 percent by 1950. This ratio fell further from about 14 percent in 1959/60 to 11 percent in 1970/71.[40] Population pressures and the military burden have pushed up the share of public consumption in the GDP from 17 percent in 1959/60 to 21 percent in 1963/64 and to 24 percent in 1969/70, thus choking off the savings potential.

It has been alleged that as much as one-half or more of available savings until the 1960s or even later were siphoned off into land speculation or upper class housing, and this gives rise to a related problem. Also, with the extreme shortage in investment funds and the preference for grandiose new schemes, much equipment replacement was neglected, and obsolete machinery was retained too long for operational efficiency.

The worsening foreign exchange crisis which was directly related to the rise in public consumption, made it difficult for many firms to obtain imports of raw materials and spare parts, and only after long delays. Capacity utilization rates consequently fell below 70 percent during the mid-1960s in a wide range of industries, especially those having to do with wood and furniture, chemicals, food and beverages, building materials, and electrical machinery and appliances. Faulty planning in terms of local supply linkages or in estimating market demand has also been to blame, as have also the technical and managerial difficulties in breaking in unfamiliar new units.[41]

A basic failure of the government's efforts to promote industrialization has been a severe misallocation of resources into sophisticated, high-prestige industries like steel and automobiles, while starving the more traditional ones like textiles. The government's motive, of course, was to broaden the industrial structure, but the more established industries would have permitted higher returns from investment and foreign exchange resources than was possible in the new areas, where the managerial and technical skill levels had not been built up to absorb efficiently the infusions of expensive and complicated equipment. Also, minimum cost production per unit of the sophisticated commodities usually requires output levels considerably in excess of Egyptian market demand; thus, diseconomies of scale resulted from the necessity of confining the output of many advanced products to low levels.

A high percentage of government-directed investments went into metallurgical establishments, these being especially capital and import intensive. An infamous example of a major metallurgical investment was the £E50 million Helwan integrated steel plant, whose output capacity was 300,000 tons per year during the 1960s. Production costs were more than 70 percent above international prices because of poor location of plant, diseconomies of scale, bad advice from the German investor associated with the project on the type of equipment ordered from abroad, overstaffing, little use of byproducts, and continual breakdowns due to the unavailability of skilled workers able to operate and maintain the equipment. The saving grace of the project was the incipient development of linkages with other emerging industries, such as pumps, metal furniture, refrigerators, tools, bicycles, automobiles, and appliances.[42]

The development of the automobile industry with technological and equipment participation by Ford and Fiat turned out to be a fiasco since Egypt was not yet in a technological position to obtain early benefits through supply linkages and, consequently, the industry remained highly import intensive. The only local components supplied in the 1960s were upholstery, side windows, paints, brake linings, clutches, batteries, and tires. The extent of the poor planning done by the government is revealed in its sudden realization in 1965 that full operation of the vehicle plants would absorb 20 percent of the total value of imports; the foreign exchange crisis led the government to cut drastically the allocations for imported vehicle parts. The result was sharply reduced production, with capacity utilization rates for the automobile and truck plants dropping to 8 and 25 percent respectively.[43]

A final factor in causing many Egyptian industries to become less competitive was the government's employment policy, combined with the relative leniency in the regulation of wages and other input prices. Firms were constantly pressured to hire more laborers than were needed, and retrenchments in staff were not permitted. Sharp rises in wages and in the prices of raw materials occurred all during the 1960s, while output prices were more tightly controlled.[44] The resulting shrinking in profit margins reduced investment flows available for the introduction of new facilities or for programs for cost reduction. The nationalizations of 1961 were accompanied by much new hiring, and the governmental pressure on maximizing employment regardless of utility continued throughout the decade. As noted earlier, only in industries such as phosphates, nitrates, tires and tubes, and cement did important technical innovations or significant increases in capacity utilization appear to lead to productivity improvements offsetting these cost increases.

Slowdown in Overall Progress

Macroeconomic indicators likewise point to a decline in economic activity after about 1963. As can be seen from Table 2.6 the average annual rate of growth in real gross domestic product has run about 5 percent over the

TABLE 2.6: Annual Rates of Growth in Real Gross Domestic Product, 1947–77

1947–52	5.2	1952–57	2.0
1956/57–1963/64	5.9	1963/64–1970/71	3.3
1971–77	6		

Sources: The 1971–77 figure is derived from recent Government of Egypt estimates. The other figures are from Bent Hansen and Karim Nashashibi, *Foreign Trade Regimes and Economic Development: Egypt* (New York: National Bureau of Economic Research, Columbia Press, 1975), pp. 12 and 109.

past thirty years; the deviation from 1952 to 1957 is due primarily to a sharp fall in cotton prices. The drop to an average of 3.3 percent from 1963/64 to 1970/71 is significant and appears related both to the destructive direct and indirect effects of the June 1967 war as well as to the suppression of foreign business and the stultification of private business.[45]

The main insight one can gain from an examination of shifts in sectoral percentage shares presented in Table 2.7 is the explosive growth in services and construction. What the table does not demonstrate is a significant early rise in importance of the industrial sector since indirect taxes were increased greatly from 1952 to 1961. Their inclusion in the GDP figures for industry exaggerates the relative growth which actually took place.[46] In any case, the table does demonstrate stability in the industry contribution to the GDP after 1964/65. Industrial output grew in constant prices by about 7 percent per year between 1952 and 1959, 8 percent from 1956 to 1961, 6.6 percent from 1961 to 1966, and 4.7 percent from 1966 to 1971.[47]

Export statistics, as presented in Table 2.8, do not demonstrate any slackening in export performance. Raw cotton remained stable, but the exports of other commodities grew steadily throughout the period, with a little slowing down only for cotton textiles. Those products which were so competitive as to be exportable continued exportable. We have seen earlier how the textile industry was starved for investment funds, and this situation may explain its slow progress.

Industrial diversification has been a principal objective of the Egyptian government during the 1960s and has been pursued, as we have seen, even beyond the point of overall benefit to the Egyptian economy. It would be nice to make an objective appraisal of how far industrial diversification has gone, but this would be difficult. It does not really appear in a descriptive listing of new or improved industrial products, such as that commencement of production has recently taken place for washing machines, transformers, electric meters, motorcycles, railway equipment, ships, metal structures, boilers, spark plugs, TV sets, recorders, transistors, and telephone equipment, and that recent substantial improvements have taken place in the quality of refrigerators, batteries, air conditioners, elevators, pumps, tubes and pipes, and metal molds.[48]

A rough impression of industrial diversification can, however, be obtained from Tables 9–12. Noteworthy in Table 2.9 is the fact that 26 out of the 42 industrial products identified as having been newly introduced from 1953/54 to 1964/65 were first produced between 1957/58 and 1960/61. Tables 2.10 and 2.11 present data on gross value-added shares of groups and branches of industry and demonstrate that higher than average growth has taken place in paper, rubber, chemicals, nonmetallic products, basic metals, simple machinery, and electrical appliances. Production of the principal industrial products from 1950 to 1970 is given in Table 2.12. Expansions were

TABLE 2.7: Sectoral Percentage Shares in GDP at Factor Costs

	1947	1952	1955/56	1960/61	1964/65	1967/68	1973	1976
Agriculture	38	33	34.4	31.5	29.7	29.0	26.3	31
Industry	13 }	13 }	13.4	20.1*	21.5	20.3	21.3	22
Electricity			0.4	0.8	1.2	1.7	1.8	1
Construction	0.4	0.4	2.3	2.8	4.7	3.8	4.2	4
Transport	3	3	6.0	7.3	8.9	5.5	5.7	7
Trade	6	7	11.0	10.4	8.6	9.3	9.2	11
Housing	19	19	7.3	6.4	3.8	5.5	4.6	3
Utilities	7	7	n.a.	0.5	0.4	0.5	0.6	0.4
Services	14	17	21.1	19.9	21.1	24.2	26.2	20

*The increase in industry's share between 1955/56 and 1960/61 is largely definitional.

Sources: The 1947 and 1952 figures are from Bent Hansen and Karim Nashashibi, Foreign Trade Regimes and Economic Development: Egypt (New York: National Bureau of Economic Research, Columbia Press, 1975), p. 12, and the 1976 figures were obtained from National Bank of Egypt, Economic Bulletin (No. 3, 1977), p. 263. The remainder are from Mabro and Radwan, op. cit., p. 47.

TABLE 2.8: Exports by Commodity Group, 1950–70 (in £E million)

	1950	1955	1960	1965	1968	1970
Raw cotton	149.8	107.4	134.7	146.2	121.1	147.8
Rice	7.6	7.3	9.8	19.8	44.9	34.2
Fruits and vegetables	2.3	4.5	9.5	12.4	11.5	29.0
Cotton textiles	4.0	7.4	18.9	47.0	52.4	53.7
Other exports	11.7	11.7	18.7	37.6	40.4	66.5
Total	175.4	138.3	191.6	263.1	270.3	331.2

Source: Hansen & Nashashibi, op. cit., p. 20.

TABLE 2.9: Introduction of New Industrial Products, 1953–54 to 1964–65

	Number	Products
1953/54	4	Pasteurized milk, preserved fruit, frozen fish, pesticides
1954/55	1	Electric wiring
1955/56	2	Tires, tubes
1956/57	2	Washing machines, radios
1957/58	6	Steel billets, steel sheets, rails, wire mesh, butagaz cylinders, cookers
1958/59	4	Pipes, air conditioners, electric meters, sewing machines
1959/60	11	Tinned fish, dacron, china, water heaters, diesel engines, cables, railway carriages, trucks, buses, cars, bicycles
1960/61	5	Ferric chloride, steel castings, heaters, switchboards, records
1961/62	3	Nitric acid, television sets, phonographs
1962/63	3	Pulp-wood, hydrochloric acid, tractors
1964/65	1	Pipes (special type)
Total	42	

Source: Mabro and Radwan, op. cit., p. 251.

TABLE 2.10: Gross Value-Added Shares of Groups of Industries (employing ten or more) 1952, 1960, 1966/67 (percentages)

Industry		1952	1960	1966/67
Group 1:	Food, beverages, tobacco, textiles, wearing apparel	64.9	58.9	55.7
Group 2:	Wood, paper, rubber, chemicals, petroleum, nonmetallic products, basic metals, metallic products	25.5	33.3	33.5
Group 3:	Nonelectric machinery, electric machinery, transport equipment	3.6	3.1	6.5
Group 4:	Furniture, printing, leather, miscellaneous	6.0	4.7	4.3
		100.0	100.0	100.0

Source: Mabro and Radwan, op. cit., p. 104.

TABLE 2.11: Gross Value-Added by Branches of Manufacturing, 1947–67

| | All Establishments | | | | Establishments Employing 10 or More | | | | | |
| | 1947 | | 1966/67 | | 1952 | | 1960 | | 1966/67 | |
Industry	£E (000s)	Percent	£E (000s)	Percent	£E (000s)	Percent	£E (000s)	Percent	£E (000s)	Percent
Food	10,513	20.7	43,983	12.1	13,553	18.2	25,617	16.4	32,696	10.7
Beverages	1,733	3.4	3,907	1.1	3,100	4.2	3,572	2.3	3,799	1.2
Tobacco	5,379	10.6	13,789	3.8	5,484	7.4	9,158	5.9	13,538	4.4
Textiles	21,812	43.0	120,556	33.2	24,722	33.2	51,977	33.3	116,376	38.1
Wearing apparel	1,057	2.1	17,440	4.8	1,400	1.9	1,560	1.0	3,774	1.2
Wood	110	0.2	3,843	1.1	155	0.2	230	0.1	1,110	0.4
Furniture	902	1.8	9,246	2.5	1,028	1.4	1,829	1.2	2,578	0.8
Paper	472	0.9	9,070	2.5	976	1.3	2,690	1.7	8,641	2.8
Printing	1,131	2.2	7,137	2.0	2,059	2.8	3,457	2.2	6,138	2.0
Leather	529	1.0	2,454	0.7	425	0.6	607	0.4	1,069	0.4
Rubber	194	0.4	2,962	0.8	275	0.4	2,617	1.7	2,886	0.9
Chemicals	2,119	4.2	39,350	10.8	5,570	7.5	17,611	11.3	38,917	12.7
Petroleum	1,034	2.0	15,953	4.4	6,358	8.5	10,957*	7.0	15,952	5.2
Nonmetallic products	1,435	2.8	15,647	4.3	3,176	4.3	8,207	5.3	12,912	4.2
Basic metals	162	0.3	12,353	3.4	1,234	1.6	7,568	4.9	11,995	3.9
Metallic products	1,709	3.4	15,525	4.3	1,283	1.7	1,985	1.3	10,032	3.3
Nonelectric machinery	16	0.0	3,939	1.1	174	0.2	688	0.4	3,401	1.1
Electric machinery	—	—	10,831	3.0	340	0.4	1,515	1.0	9,888	3.2
Transport equipment	249	0.5	9,780	2.7	2,336	3.1	2,706	1.7	6,496	2.1
Miscellaneous	269	0.5	5,088	1.4	865	1.2	1,413	0.9	3,493	1.1
	50,735		362,843		74,513		155,964		305,691	

Source: Mabro and Radwan, op. cit., p. 101.

TABLE 2.12: Main Items of Industrial Production, 1950–70

Item	Unit	1950	1960	1963	1965	1968	1970
Crude petroleum	,000 Cubic Meters	2,349	3,609	6,153	7,129	9,890	18,945
Phosphate	,000 Tons	397	566	612	594	1,441	582
Manganese	,000 Tons	152	286	49	182	4	4
Common salt	,000 Tons	567	522	392	494	622	444
Iron ore	,000 Tons	n.a.	239	489	507	447	451
Limestone	,000 Cubic Meters	n.a.	2,813	3,185	3,051	4,000	5,500
Dairy products	,000 Tons	5	105	128	140	152	163
Refined sugar	,000 Tons	n.a.	338	356	400	380	547
Cotton seed oil	,000 Tons	91	104	139	148	92	137
Rice bleached	,000 Tons	842	1,200	754	900	1,208	1,462
Starch	,000 Tons	4	9	12	12	16	15
Glucose	,000 Tons	4	26	31	33	33	38
Alcohol	Million Liters	15	17	19	19	27	32
Beer	Million Liters	13	14	20	24	21	24
Cotton yarn	,000 Tons	49	102	123	138	157	164
Cotton fabrics	,000 Tons	n.a.	64	80	89	102	110

TABLE 2.12: (Continued)

Artificial silk thread & fabrics	,000 Tons	3	21	22	20	21	13
Woolen yarn & fabrics	,000 Tons	3	10	17	19	12	11
Jute yarn & fabrics	,000 Tons	3	25	50	34	53	52
Ordinary paper & cardboard	,000 Tons	n.a.	49	95	106	116	125
Cars, trucks, and buses	Number of	—	1,107	5,942	5,613	1,990	5,123
Car tires and tubes	,000 Units	n.a.	485	519	1,201	1,832	1,566
Sulphuric acid	,000 Tons	n.a.	103	113	194	260	30
Caustic soda	,000 Tons	38	4	18	19	20	20
Super phosphate	,000 Tons	4	188	164	252	306	437
Lime nitrates	,000 Tons	69	257	261	278	168	387
Soap	,000 Tons	n.a.	80	98	97	154	136
Asphalt	,000 Tons	80	112	143	134	143	59
Butagas	,000 Tons	n.a.	20	39	58	42	10
Other refined petroleum products	,000 Tons	2,111	3,998	5,950	7,632	6,184	3,188
Glazed glass	,000 Tons	n.a.	12	16	12	14	15
Iron products	,000 Tons	n.a.	340	422	378	473	434
Portland cement	,000 Tons	1,020	1,903	1,723	1,777	2,309	3,684

Sources: Federation of Egyptian Industries, *Yearbook 1969*, *Yearbook 1972* (Cairo: General Organization for the Government Printing Office), and National Bank of Egypt, *Economic Bulletin* (No. 3, 1966), Table 6/1 B.

most significant in cement, super phosphates, lime nitrates, petroleum, glucose, dairy products, beer, yarns and fabrics, and tires and tubes.[49] The drawback in the use of such a table of long-term duration is the focus on the more established products. Production statistics are not available for the more sophisticated commodities until a couple of years or so after they have become established.

In this examination of the positive and negative aspects of the three previous growth phases of recent Egyptian economic history, the interaction between foreign investor participation and Egyptian enterprise has been emphasized. Results were unsatisfactory up to 1920, as either Egyptian efforts were vigorous but were stymied by foreign hostility, as happened before 1850, or foreign involvement was substantial but Egyptian enterprise was lethargic. In the third phase, from 1956 to 1971, results were also unsatisfactory as the suppression of both foreign and local enterprise contributed to a decline in the efficiency and competitiveness of much of Egyptian industry and a slowdown in overall economic progress.

The period from 1920 to 1956 was more satisfactory than the other two in that the beginnings of vigorous Egyptian entrepreneurial activity were combined with some positive joint venture activity on the part of foreign investors. During that time, Egyptians eschewed autarchy, and foreign investors were neither hostile to Egyptian development nor engaged in enclave type projects. The vigorous activities of the emerging Egyptian entrepreneurs, and the fairly numerous instances of cooperation between foreign and Egyptian business promoted many simple industrial ventures and stimulated moderate overall economic growth.

NOTES

1. A good summary of the different aspects of Ali's revolution appears in Charles Issawi, *Egypt In Revolution—An Economic Analysis* (New York: Oxford University Press, 1963), pp. 21–24; and in "Egypt Since 1800: A Study in Lopsided Development," *The Journal of Economic History,* Vol. 31 (March 1961), pp. 1–27.

2. An account of the range of industrial activity under Ali together with high opinions on the skills acquired during that period is given in Moustafa Fahmy, *La Revolution de l'Industrie en Egypte et Ses Consequences Sociales au 19ᵉ Siecle (1800–1850),* (Leiden: E. J. Brill, 1954).

3. See cited works of Issawi, and Fahmy, op. cit., pp. 21–47.

4. See Fahmy, op. cit., pp. 72–111, and Robert Mabro and Samir Radwan, *The Industrialization of Egypt, 1939–1973—Policy and Performance* (New York: Oxford University Press, 1976), pp. 17–18.

5. The Franco-Ottoman Treaty of 1861 raised the uniform ad valorem import duty from 5 to 8 percent. There were later exceptions on alcohol, sugar, timber, petroleum, and live animals to the extent of 10 or 15 percent. The 8 percent rate remained in force until 1930.

6. The total number of foreigners rose from about 3,000 in 1836 to over 68,000 in 1878 and to 221,000 in 1907. See Issawi, op. cit., p. 29.

7. See Issawi, op. cit., p. 39, and Donald C. Mead, *Growth and Structural Change In the Egyptian Economy* (Homewood, Illinois: Richard D. Irwin, 1967), p. 178.

8. Mabro and Radwan, op. cit., p. 25.

9. See cited Issawi article, pp. 12–13; and Mabro and Radwan, op. cit., pp. 24–26.

10. A detailed account of the animosity created by the successive setting of prices by foreign-controlled firms at levels which allegedly far exceeded cost trends appears in Robert L. Tignor, "The Egyptian Revolution of 1919: New Directions In the Egyptian Economy," *Middle Eastern Studies,* Vol. 12 (October 1976), pp. 44–46.

11. See Mabro and Radwan, op. cit., pp. 50–62. A table showing the calculated rates of effective protection for selected industries for 1959 appears there on p. 61.

12. Quoted from Bank Misr's charter. See Marius Deeb, "Bank Misr and the Emergence of the Local Bourgeoisie In Egypt," *Middle Eastern Studies,* Vol. 12 (October 1976), p. 70.

13. These Federation statistics appear in ibid., pp. 75, 78.

14. See ibid., pp. 70–71, and Tignor, op. cit., p. 58.

15. Deeb, op. cit., p. 75.

16. Deeb, in ibid., p. 77, also points out that Bank Misr participated in new companies dominated by resident foreigners. Most of the purely Egyptian enterprises that the Bank continued to sponsor, such as producers of tobacco and cigarettes, had much less capital than the joint ventures created with the participation of overseas capital.

17. Mabro and Radwan, op. cit., p. 28. Bank Misr became a much less significant force for Egyptian industrialization after 1939 with the appointment of a new governor who did not believe in Bank Misr funds being used to promote new industrial plants. However, it continued to finance and reinforce existing Misr companies and to participate in several mixed enterprises launched by the government, such as a steel mill, a chemical plant, and a hotel company. See Deeb, op. cit., pp. 79–80.

18. See Deeb, op. cit., p. 79, and Issawi, *Egypt In Revolution,* p. 89.

19. Egypt's training programs for technicians and skilled workers during the 1940s and early 1950s is described in Frederick Harbison, *Human Resources for Egyptian Enterprise* (New York: McGraw Hill Book Co., Inc., 1958), pp. 47–57.

20. Issawi, op. cit., pp. 87–88.

21. See Tignor, op. cit., p. 48, and Mead, op. cit., p. 249.

22. See Harbison, op. cit., pp. 56–57.

23. Suez Canal Authority, *Annual Report, 1959* (Cairo: 1960), and Issawi, op. cit., p. 213.

24. These figures are very rough estimates. See Tignor, op. cit., p. 47, and Issawi, op. cit., p. 238.

25. Issawi, op. cit., p. 178.

26. Ibid., p. 236.

27. See especially Patrick O'Brien, *The Revolution in Egypt's Economic System* (New York: Oxford University press, 1966), p. 13.

28. Mabro and Radwan, op. cit., p. 29, and Mazdi El-Kammash, *Economic Development and Planning in Egypt* (New York: Praeger Special Studies, 1963), p. 213.

29. Issawi, "Egypt Since 1800," pp. 17–18.

30. See O'Brien, op. cit., Chapter III.

31. A summary account of these new laws appears in Issawi, op. cit., p. 53.

32. Suez Canal Authority, *Annual Report, 1960* (Cairo: 1961).

33. See Mead, op. cit., p. 50, and Issawi, op. cit., p. 57.

34. Issawi, op. cit., pp. 89–90.

35. Details of the different measures of nationalization are given in ibid., pp. 58–62.

36. See Mead, op. cit., p. 53; Bent Hansen and Karim Nashashibi, *Foreign Trade Regimes and Economic Development: Egypt* (New York: National Bureau of Economic Research, Columbia University Press, 1975), p. 9; and Mabro and Radwan, op. cit., p. 96.

37. Some aspects of Egypt's overall performance in exportation, including manufacturing, are presented in Mabro and Radwan, op. cit., pp. 212–21.

38. Examples of high or growing productivity in selected Egyptian industries are given in Issawi, op. cit., pp. 325, 328; Mead, op. cit., p. 105; and Hansen and Nashashibi, op. cit., pp. 255, 268–69, 271.

39. Mabro and Radwan, op. cit., pp. 147, 183.

40. See Mabro and Radwan, op. cit., p. 20; Hansen and Nashahibi, op. cit., pp. 314–15; and Albert L. Gray, Jr., "Egypt's Ten Year Economic Plan, 1073–1982," *Middle East Journal,* Vol. 30 (Winter 1976), pp. 38–41.

41. An appraisal of the degree of capacity underutilization by principal industrial activity appears in Mabro and Radwan, op. cit., pp. 157–63.

42. A caustic view of the Helwan Steel venture is presented in Hansen and Nashashibi, op. cit., pp. 285–94. A more sympathetic view, because of the dynamic training possibilities for associated industries, is given in Harbison, op. cit., p. 28.

43. See Hansen and Nashashibi, op. cit., pp. 297–304.

44. Examples of cost escalation through rises in import prices outstripping productivity improvements appear in Mead, op. cit., pp. 117, 124, and Hansen and Nashashibi, op. cit., pp. 95–99, 236, 246.

45. Mabro and Radwan believe that published growth statistics may outstate the actual rates of growth by some 15 or 20 percent due to various biases, the most important of which is the use of deflators which do not reflect the full extent of price increases. See their op. cit., pp. 41–43.

46. I am indebted to Charles Issawi for this observation. See his op. cit., pp. 115–16.

47. See Richard F. Nyrop, *Area Handbook For Egypt* (Washington, D.C.: Foreign Area Studies, 1976), p. 290.

48. See, for example, Government of Egypt, *Egypt's Industrial Revolution in 20 Years 1952–1972* (Cairo: 1973), pp. 167–68, and annual reports of the Federation of Egyptian Industries.

49. Mabro and Radwan, from whom most of the data on industrial diversification were obtained, offer the overall appraisal that progress in industrial diversification was more significant before 1960 than afterwards. See their op. cit., p. 106.

3

EVOLUTION OF LEGAL FRAMEWORK

We have seen in the last chapter that the Egyptian government took hostile actions against foreign investors from several countries, and that restrictions on Egyptian private enterprise were tightened during the same period, i.e., from about 1956 to 1971. A turnaround in governmental attitudes toward foreign investment has taken place beginning about 1971. A legislative breakthrough occurred in 1974 with the promulgation of a comprehensive foreign investment code. This code contains many new positive features. A dialogue ensued almost immediately with foreign investors on the need for additional clarification and the removal of remaining impediments. The government followed through with the 1977 amendment and other regulatory changes, which have vastly improved the legal framework for doing business in Egypt.

THE TURNAROUND IN GOVERNMENTAL ATTITUDES TOWARDS FOREIGN INVESTMENT

As we have seen, the Egyptian government had taken over the properties of British, French, and Belgian investors prior to the July 1961 nationalization laws that resulted in further takeovers of foreign investors' property. The year 1961 probably represents the nadir in relations between the government and foreign business; some slight improvement took place during the ensuing decade, with a mellowing taking place after the October 1973 war.

The relatively favorable foreign investment laws No. 156 and 475 of 1953 and 1954 had never been revoked despite the sweeping governmental takeovers of foreign businesses. The National Charter of 1962 clarified the government's current attitude to new foreign investments by ranking foreign private investments after foreign grants and loans in terms of priority consideration. After careful assessment and screening, foreign investments would be welcomed in critical industries requiring new technologies and skills not available domestically. While foreign participation in management and unconditional repatriation of profits would be accorded, there would also be careful government control over the firms' operations in Egypt.

Law No. 32 of 1966, establishing general organizations and public sector companies, envisaged the joint participation of foreign private capital with domestic public capital. The joint ventures would operate in accordance with special governmental regulations.[1]

Despite these slight improvements in governmental attitudes, foreign investments remained largely confined to the petroleum and pharmaceutical sectors, and the roughly £E8 million in new foreign investments, which had entered during the 1950s, were probably not significantly exceeded during the 1960s.

Following the elevation of Anwar el-Sadat to be President of Egypt in May 1971, the Rectification Movement was launched to define a new relationship between the government and the people.[2] The movement was an attempt to remove the suspicions engendered by the widespread sequestrations and arrests of the Nasser era through reasserting the sovereignty of law and clarifying the legal rights of persons. There was a recognition that, if the domestic or foreign private sector was to make the fullest possible contribution to Egypt's economic development, an environment in which individuals and firms would feel greater freedom, confidence, and security had to be established.

A new constitution was proclaimed on September 11, 1971, based upon respect for "individual freedoms" and the "rule of law." Protection of private property is guaranteed through Articles 34 and 35, prohibiting sequestration, expropriation, or nationalization except when the public interest is involved, and fair compensation is to be made in accordance with law. A Supreme Constitutional Court was established to judge the constitutionality of laws and regulations and to render authoritative interpretations of legislative texts.[3]

Also significant, at this stage, was Egypt's adherence to several international agreements. Law No. 90 of 1971 endorsed Egypt's adherence to the Convention on the Settlement of Investment Disputes administered by the World Bank. Presidential Decree 109 of 1972 approved Egypt's adherence to the Agreement for the Establishment of the Arab Organization for the Safeguarding of Investments, and Egypt also later joined the Agreement on Investment and Movement of Arab Capital among Arab countries.

The most significant piece of legislation, during this initial period of warming-up in the government's attitude towards foreign business, was Law No. 65 of 1971, concerning the investment of Arab funds and the Free Zones. While this law specifically had to do with Arab investment funds, Article 18 stated that other foreign investors would enjoy the benefits and guarantees provided by the law, following the approval of the Cabinet and the President.

Among the privileges and guarantees included in the 1971 law are the following: 1) capital repatriation is allowed after five years in the original currency and at the prevailing exchange rate, 2) remittance of profits is permissible at the prevailing exchange rate, 3) proceeds of foreign currency earnings can be used for remittances or for payment of needed imported materials and capital equipment, 4) there is to be fair compensation in the event of nationalization or expropriation, 5) profits are exempted from taxation for five years, and 6) the General Authority for Investment of Arab Funds and the Free Zones was established to prepare lists of the types of projects in which foreign investment is invited to participate. Priority is given to projects aimed at exportation or stimulation of tourism, projects requiring advanced technical expertise, patents, or trademarks, and projects tending to reduce import requirements. The Authority is also responsible for approving investment applications and facilitates the obtaining of the various clearances from other government departments.

A major omission in the Law was the fact that imports of capital equipment for approved projects were not exempted from customs duties. This omission was remedied in the area of tourism by Law No. 1 of 1973, concerning hotel and touristic establishments. All items imported for construction, renovation, replacement, and spare parts throughout the life of the project were exempted from customs duties. This law also extended for the first time to Egyptian investors the same privileges and exemptions granted to foreigners.[4]

The Transformation of the Psychological Environment

The October War of 1973 may in time be classified as the most important event in Egypt since World War II. Politically, the decisiveness of the initial breakthrough into the Sinai and the reasonably favorable military and political outcome removed the sense of inferiority under which the Egyptians had been laboring and made it psychologically possible for them to take courageous steps to move towards peace in the Middle East. At the same time, the initiation of peace moves has greatly improved the overall foreign investment climate and raised hopes for greater long-term political stability. In the economic sphere, the Arab confrontation with the United States during and just after the war set the stage during the fall and winter for the OPEC countries to bring about a four-fold increase in petroleum prices. The result was an unprecedented shift in purchasing power benefiting a few countries; the tremors within the international financial system are still continuing.

At the domestic economic level, the war boosted the morale of Egyptian policy-makers and strengthened the bonds between the government and the people. The government felt emboldened to move vigorously to improve the overall environment for rapid economic growth and for attracting greater domestic and foreign business participation. The principles underlying the new economic strategy were enunciated in President Sadat's October Working Paper, which was presented to the People's Assembly in April 1974 and approved in a national referendum in May. This strategy, known as the open-door policy, calls for a movement towards a more "mixed" and less regimented economy in which both the local, private sector and foreign investments are called upon to play a greater role along with the existing public sector in accelerating Egypt's economic development. The strategy involves decentralization of decision-making in state-owned enterprises; the liberalization of private business activities in capital formation and trade; the restructuring of the government's investment program; the provision for adequate incentives to stimulate foreign and domestic private investments; and the restoration of adequate public services and an economic infrastructure to improve the economy's absorptive capacity.[5]

During an Egyptian investment seminar sponsored by the National Foreign Trade Council on September 29, 1978, Gamal el Nazar, the Minister of State for Economic Affairs and Economic Cooperation, stressed the significance of the October Working Paper and its approval by the People's Assembly and a national referendum. He stated that these actions pointed to the long-term character of the open-door policy. Since the policy has been overwhelmingly approved by the people, it is independent of how long the present government lasts, and foreign investors should have no doubts that it would survive any change of government.

THE 1974 FOREIGN INVESTMENT CODE: POSITIVE FEATURES AND REMAINING IMPEDIMENTS

The approval of the October Working Paper in a national referendum in May 1974 was followed in June by the promulgation of Law No. 43, "Concerning the Investment of Arab and Foreign Funds and the Free Zones." This comprehensive code created a new legal framework designed to encourage foreign investors to make their capital and technology available to Egypt as an integral part of its efforts to promote accelerated growth. However, there remained several major impediments in the Law. Since this code is the most important piece of legislation still affecting the operations of foreign investors, it is analyzed in detail below. The full text of Law No. 43, as amended by Law No. 32 of 1977, is provided in the Appendix.

Principal Provisions of the 1974 Code

I divide this analysis of the 1974 foreign investment code into four major sections, namely: Joint Venture Approach, Repatriation and Remittances of Funds, Fields of Authorized Investment, and Incentives and Guarantees.

Joint Venture Approach

Article 4 stipulates that capital invested under the provisions of this law shall take the form of participation with public or private Egyptian capital. Foreign investment in banks engaging in local currency transactions can not exceed 49 percent of the total equity. The 1974 law does not stipulate a strict minimum percentage of local equity in other fields. Some local participation is required in branches of foreign investment banks and merchant banks, and the basic spirit of the law strongly suggests the desirability of some local participation elsewhere. Clause C of Article 4, however, stipulates that "the Authority's Board of Directors, by a two-thirds majority vote of its members, may approve the investment of Arab or foreign capital without local participation in the other fields."

Repatriation and Remittance of Funds

The repatriation of capital is allowed after five years in five equal annual installments at the rate of exchange prevailing at the time of transfer. Article 21 of the law goes on to state that the value of the capital allowed to be repatriated shall be the original registered value plus a percentage to be fixed by the Authority to match any appreciation which may have occurred in the value of such capital.

Article 22 states that "projects realizing self sufficiency in their foreign currency needs, whose earnings from visible exports cover all their required imports of machinery, equipment, production imputs and materials, and which pay for all foreign currency loans and interest thereon, shall be permitted to transfer their annual net profits." The original article then went on to state that "basic projects with major significance to the national economy, where no exports are contemplated, are permitted to transfer the net profits from the foreign investment in full." Originally, there had also been a clause specifying that the government was under no obligation to allow the transfer of profits from projects of which the total value is less than £E50,000.

As in the 1971 law, permission may be had to utilize foreign currency earnings to open a foreign currency account with an authorized Egyptian bank to pay for needed imported materials and equipment and for payment of interest and principal on foreign loans.

Fields of Authorized Investment

Article 3 states that foreign investment "shall be for the purpose of realizing the objectives of economic and social development within the framework of the state's general policy and national plan, provided that the investment is made in projects in need of international expertise in the spheres of modern development or in projects requiring foreign capital." The General Authority for Foreign Investment is charged with preparing lists of the types of activities and projects in which foreign investment is invited to participate and, as was also the case under the 1971 law, screens investment application, approves remittances of net profits, and helps to obtain the necessary permits from other departments.

Article 4 excludes housing projects from the field of general foreign investment; such projects may be undertaken only with Arab capital. The fields for authorized foreign investment are otherwise very broad: the reclamation of barren land, livestock, water, and urban development, and "industrialization, mining, energy, tourism, transportation and other fields." Special priority, however, shall be given to "those projects which are designed to generate exports, encourage tourism, or reduce the need to import basic commodities, as well as to projects which require advanced technical expertise or which make use of patents or trademarks of world-wide reputation."

Incentives and Guarantees

Law No. 43 considerably expanded the scope of incentives and guarantees. Article 16 states that "projects shall be exempted from the tax on commercial and industrial profits and the taxes appendent thereto; likewise distributed profits shall be exempted from the tax on the income from movable capital." Exemption from the annual proportional stamp duty is also specifically provided. In a major improvement on the 1971 law, the period of exemption does not start with the date of entry of the capital, but with the first tax year following commencement of production or operations.

The period of tax exemption under Article 16 is five years and may be extended to eight years depending on "the nature of the project, its geographic location, its importance to economic development, the volume of its capital, and the extent to which it participates in exploiting natural resources and increasing exports." The tax exemptions are also available over the same periods to reinvested profits. The exemptions are only applicable, however, as long as the profits are not, as a consequence, subject to taxation in the investor's home country or in any other country.

Interest due on foreign loans for the project, whether concluded by the foreign investor or the Egyptian participant, shall be exempt from Egyptian taxation. The original Article 17 had provided vaguely that "the profits distributed by a project shall be exempted from the general tax on income up to a maximum of 5% of the taxpayer's share in the invested capital." A 1977 amendment made clear, what was perhaps already implied, that this Article applied after the expiration of the tax exemption period established under Article 16.

A new feature omitted in the 1971 law, but incorporated in the 1973 law on touristic establishments, is the duty exemptions on imported equipment and materials. Such imports for the start-up or current operations of projects also do not require licenses.

Article 7 states unconditionally that "projects may not be nationalized or confiscated. The assets of such projects cannot be seized, blocked, confiscated or sequestered except by judicial procedures." Disputes are to be settled in a manner to be agreed upon with the investor, or within the framework of international conventions, or by a three-member arbitration board.

Approved projects, even when carried out as a joint venture with a public company, are deemed to belong to the private sector. Consequently, the laws and regulations applicable to the public sector and its employees do not apply, such as those concerning labor representation on the board of directors, profit sharing, and limitations on directors' salaries. However, the statutes of the companies must provide for some labor participation in management, and company rules must specify some distribution of profits to employees.

The provisions regarding the establishment of foreign investment operations in free zones offer a wide range of favorable incentives, including freedom from customs duties and almost total relief from corporate taxes on profits for an unlimited time.

Remaining Impediments

Some of the key provisions of Law No. 43 were ill-defined, but a sufficient basis for attracting foreign investors would have been established if regulations had been issued on the necessary clarifications. The bureaucracy, however, did not act decisively and flexibly in formulating clarifying regulations or in interpreting the existing law. As a result, debate quickly ensued on the need to change Law No. 43 itself.

The foreign business community played an active part in this debate. The Egypt-U.S. Business Council held its inaugural meeting in Cairo in October 1975; it was attended by 40 American business executives, 20 Egyptian executives, and six Egyptian government ministers. This meeting focused on the impediments to investing in Egypt. A task force from the American section was formed and subsequently made a survey of over 50 U.S. companies—and a few Canadian and European firms—with current or potential operations in Egypt. A report, highlighting the critical problem areas and developing recommendations on ways to attract greater foreign investment, was presented to the Egyptian government in March 1976.[6] A foreign investment orientation seminar, sponsored by the Council in New York that same year, gave the sixteen Egyptian government participants an additional opportunity to obtain foreign business feedback on Egypt's investment laws. A Business International round-table discussion in Cairo in December 1975 and a series of seminars by the Fund for Multinational Management Education, the U.S.-Arab Chamber of Commerce, the American Management Association, and other business organizations and institutions also served to make clear the reactions of American businessmen. In late 1976 the Egyptian government became firmly convinced of the need to eliminate the major inadequacies and ambiguities of the 1974 law; it accordingly circulated drafts of proposed changes at the later seminars and separately to several international organizations.

All foreign investors canvassed have stressed that the single most important difficulty with the original version of Law No. 43 was the determination of the applicable exchange rate.[7] According to the law, foreign capital enters at the official rate, and the repatriation of capital is to be made at the "prevailing rate." The law does not define which of several prevailing rates is meant, and is silent on the rate at which dividends will be remitted. Substantial foreign exchange losses, therefore, appear automatic and there is, in any case, a high degree of uncertainty about future receipts on conversions from Egyptian currency.

The next most important impediment to foreign investor interest is the bias against import substitution projects in terms of profit repatriation rights and foreign exchange availability. Export-oriented projects have little trouble except for the occasional long delays experienced in getting either type of transaction approved by the authorities.[8] Foreign investors proposing projects without export potential rarely have any assurance regarding their rights of profit repatriation. Not many import substitution projects qualify as to the other criterion for assured profit repatriation, namely as "basic projects with major significance to the national economy." The term "basic" is not at all clear. There is the same lack of assurance that there will be adequate foreign exchange forthcoming to finance the import of needed components and spare parts, since the permission to open a foreign currency account to finance such purchases mentions the receipt of foreign exchange earnings from the project, but makes no other provision for financing if such earnings are not available. There is even the negative statement of Article 15 dismissing governmental concern in this area: "there shall be no obligation on the part of the government to provide the foreign currency necessary for the importing operations beyond the bank accounts mentioned in the preceding Article.[9] Since most prospective investors are interested in Egypt because of its large potential domestic market, and Egypt is not such a good export base, this bias against import substitution projects has stifled much foreign investor interest.

A major ambiguity concerns the tax holiday provisions. Forfeiture of the tax holiday could occur if a foreign tax authority imposed a tax on the Egyptian earnings of such projects "as a consequence" of the tax holiday. This is by no means a negligible possibility, since many home investor countries do not have tax sparing provisions to prevent the elimination of the incentive effect of tax holiday schemes in host developing countries. The tax holiday provisions also did not specify clearly what taxes the exemptions apply to. In particular, there was a serious concern whether there is an exemption from the Egyptian General Tax on Income, even during the initial five to eight-year tax holiday period, in view of the silence on that particular tax in the relevant Article 16, while Article 17 on the additional 5 percent exemption (implicitly, post tax holiday) did refer specifically to such a tax.[10] There is also a fear that the tax holiday exemptions may not apply to other taxes already effective, or those that may be introduced in the future.

I will conclude this by no means exhaustive description of the impediments of Law No. 43 by mentioning the valuation provision on capital repatriation. Some foreign investors maintain that leaving the valuation of the repatriated capital to the discretion of a possibly unresponsive Authority could substantially weaken the value of capital repatriation after a highly inflationary period.

THE 1977 AMENDMENT AND OTHER REGULATORY CHANGES

Despite the several major impediments outlined above, the 1974 law represented a comprehensive effort to woo foreign investors. The dialogue between Egyptian government officials and foreign businessmen during 1975 and 1976 had served a useful role in highlighting the various impediments. The Egyptian government showed that it was quite responsive to many of the concerns expressed by foreign investors when it issued on June 19, 1977, Law No. 32 of 1977, and made several other changes in regulations. Law No. 32 was enacted to amend Law No. 43 of 1974. This amendment and the other regulatory changes are described below.

The 1977 Amendment

To eliminate the confusion arising from the applicable foreign exchange rate and to reduce the possibility of foreign exchange losses in capital repatriation and profit remittances, a substitute second section of Article 2 was added. This section uses the same definition for the foreign exchange rate on entries and departures of capital in stating that "invested capital shall be transferred to, and exported from, the Arab Republic of Egypt, and profits generated therefrom shall be transferred in foreign currency abroad . . . at the highest rate prevailing and declared for free foreign currency by the competent Egyptian authorities." An additional section applies the preceding section to land and property which are an integral part of the assets of approved projects. The former denial of a government obligation to allow profit remittances from projects valued at less than £E50,000 has been deleted.

The prejudice against import substitution projects was substantially reduced by amending the second section of Article 22 as follows: "projects that are basically not export oriented, and that limit the country's need for imports, shall be permitted to transfer, in whole *or in part* [author's emphasis], their net profits at the highest rate prevailing and declared for foreign currency within the limits approved by the Authority and subject to currency regulations in force." The government still insists that full remittance of profits on import substitution projects is not guaranteed and that the percentage of profits allowed to be remitted must be determined on a "case by case" basis. The government has been unwilling to offer any criteria by which this determination will be made.[11]

An amendment to Article 14 somewhat increases foreign exchange availabilities for approved projects by authorizing foreign investors to also fund their foreign currency accounts through purchases from local banks or with the proceeds of sales to the local market in foreign currency.

Amendments to Article 21 expand the ability of a foreign investor to divest through enlarging the definition of what is considered invested capital and through authorizing immediate use of all amounts accrued in a project's foreign exchange account, and through the sale of company shares on the Egyptian stock exchange.

Three new fields have been specifically opened up to foreign investment by amendments to Article 3. These new fields comprise construction activities outside the existing agricultural area and cities; construction contracting in which there is at least a 50 percent minimum Egyptian equity; and technical consulting urgently needed for other approved projects.

The range of tax and duty exemptions has been increased. Most importantly, profits during the tax holiday period are now specifically exempted from "the general tax on income." This exemption, however, is now specifically forfeited if project income is subject to "similar taxation in the investor's home country or in the country to which income is transferred." The tax holiday is now also applicable to undistributed profits set aside for special reserves or to be distributed after the exemption period has elapsed. The exemption period for land reclamation, reconstruction and, establishment of new outlying cities is now ten to fifteen years. Deferred or installment payments on customs and other duties may be authorized on imports of capital equipment, construction material, and components needed to establish approved projects. The tax burden on expatriates has been alleviated by an addition to Article 20 stating that "all payments subject to the Employment Earnings Tax, such as wages, salaries, bonuses, or other similar payments made to foreign employees by projects established according to the provisions of this Law, shall be exempt from the General Tax on Income."

Law No. 86 of 1974 had been enacted to provide projects funded by local currency with incentives similar to those made available to joint ventures under Law No. 43. As no implementing body was ever established, the provisions of this Law remained unimplemented. An addition to Article 6 of the 1977 amendments stipulates that the Authority is also responsible for projects "established in any of the areas set forth in Article 3 entirely with Egyptian capital and owned by Egyptian nationals, and [the projects] shall enjoy the privileges and exemptions set forth in Articles 9, 14, 15, 16, 17 and 18." Domestic investors are thus accorded benefits substantially similar to those accorded foreign investors.[12] Since an important element of a favorable foreign investment climate is stimulation of private enterprise generally, the new generous treatment of Egyptian enterprise is welcomed by foreign investors.

Changes in Other Laws and Regulations

The foreign investment climate has been improved by a number of other changes in laws and regulations promulgated between 1974 and 1977. Foreign exchange availability has been increased for Egyptian investors through Law No. 97 of 1976. Egyptians possessing foreign exchange on their own, however, obtained in the past, may use such funds to buy imports from the list of approved parallel market goods without converting their currency through the Egyptian banking system. A preferential exchange rate had been established in the summer of 1973 at 50 percent above the official rate; this premium was raised to 65 percent in February 1976. This preferential exchange rate applies to tourist purchases, the currency brought in by returning Egyptians, the transfer abroad of interests and profits, and the proceeds of nontraditional exports. During the spring of 1976, the government also decided to apply the preferential rate rather than the official rate for the calculation of import duties on many consumer items, covering one-fifth of Egypt's imports.

Prior to January 1, 1976, industrial enterprises in Egypt were subject to a high degree of control in their planning and operations by General Organizations for industrial subsectors. Law No. 111 of September 18, 1975, abolished these General Organizations, and, in their place, established Supreme Sector Councils in January 1976. Later implementing regulations gave the public companies authority to arrange for their own importation of raw materials and components, and for the receipt of foreign exchange and finance from banks. This measure increased the decentralization of decision-making and loosened the public sector grip on the economy. The Supreme Councils do not interfere in day-to-day managerial decision-making as was frequently the case with the General Organizations; they rather collect statistics and review the broad outlines of companies' budgets and investment programs. Plant managers now have direct contact with the relevant ministries, where, it must be admitted, cumbersome procedures and long delays are often experienced. Major investment decisions and the determination of output targets for the important commodities are still made at the ministerial level.[13]

A decree had been issued in June 1975 allowing Egyptian individuals to purchase shares in public sector companies up to a limit of $24,000.

Law No. 120 of 1975 and other regulations have been issued permitting the banks greater flexibility and autonomy in their day-to-day operations in such important areas as salaries, foreign exchange dealings, and the setting of interest rates. A late 1976 decree permitted Egyptians to open checking and savings accounts in foreign currencies without questions being asked about the source of the money deposited. These new laws, together with the positive provisions of Law No. 43 of 1974, have set the stage for the entry of many foreign banks, both on "offshore" and joint venture bases, as will be discussed in the next chapter.

Other laws which strengthened the role of Egyptian private enterprise include Law No. 93 of 1974, authorizing Egyptians from the private sector to act as commercial agents for foreign firms.

A 1961 law had required that agents for foreign firms be companies in which the government's share was no less than 25 percent. New legislation in September 1975 significantly reduced the monopoly over foreign trade formerly enjoyed by the state trading companies. Private companies became free to import directly all commodities, except 28 key items. The 28 items which continue to be handled by the public sector include wheat, flour, fuels, fertilizers, wool, and jute.[14] In a move to assure protection for local industries, the government drew up a list in March 1978 of more than 80 commodities for which special import licenses are required. These commodities include telephone cables, agricultural tractors, pumps, artificial leather, plastic containers, cosmetics, toothpaste, cardboard boxes, and textiles.

To encourage private savings and investment, the government reopened the Cairo and Alexandria stock exchanges and, in May 1977, raised the rate of interest and made earnings from savings tax exempt. New rules were issued, effective November 1, 1977, on the operations of the stock exchanges, with stock brokers being permitted to open free currency accounts with approved banks to buy and sell securities in free foreign currencies. Interest rates were raised again in June 1978 from 8–9 to 9–11 percent (plus 3/8 percent commission).

Some foreign investors feel the need for further legal improvements in such areas as trademarks and patents, taxation, and labor. Further steps to revitalize the Egyptian private sector would also be welcome, such as the promised sale of 49 percent of the shares in some public sector companies to private Egyptians. There still remain serious impediments for import substitution projects not assured foreign exchange availability or full profit repatriation. On balance, however, the Egyptian government has made major strides from 1974 to 1977 in addressing the major legal problems brought up during dialogues with foreign investors. The present legal framework for doing business in Egypt is probably better than average for host developing countries and can definitely be classified as attractive. Given the political difficulties of introducing change in Egypt's legal system and given the responsive character of the changes which have already been made, not much further legal or regulatory change is expected. In any case, the legal framework is no longer a serious obstacle to the entry of foreign investment, and foreign investor attention is rather directed to the environmental factors discussed in Chapter 5.

NOTES

1. A brief summary of the 1962 National Charter and a reference to the 1966 Law appears in Robert E. Driscoll, P. F. Hayek, Farouk A. Zaki, *Foreign Investment in Egypt: An Analysis of Critical Factors with Emphasis on the Foreign Investment Code* (New York: Fund for Multinational Management Education, 1978), p. 7.

2. The rationale for the Rectification Movement is well presented in Delwin A. Roy, *Private Industry Sector Development in Egypt: An Analysis of Trends, 1973–1977,* Report to the Special Interagency Task Force Reviewing the U.S. Security Supporting Assistance Program for Egypt (Washington, D.C.: USAID, January 1978), p. 4.

3. Excerpts of the 1971 Constitution are contained in Driscoll, op. cit., p. 8.

4. A good summary of the 1971 and 1973 laws is given in Driscoll, ibid., pp. 9–14. The text of all important Egyptian legislation is given in various issues of National Bank of Egypt, *Economic Bulletin.*

5. See both Roy, op. cit., pp. 5–6, and Driscoll, op. cit., pp. 9–10, for a description of the economic philosophy underlying the October Working Paper.

6. See Egypt-U.S. Business Council, *Report on Foreign Investment in Egypt* (Washington, D.C.: 1976).

7. An extensive discussion of the exchange rate problem appears in ibid., pp. 8–14. See also Roy, op. cit., p. 19.

8. Foreign exchange availability is, however, sometimes a problem with export-oriented projects during the start-up period. Driscoll et al. have some reports from investors in export-oriented projects who worry whether their profit repatriation rights are automatic or whether they are subject to the discretion of the Authority. The 1977 Amendment changed the phrase "may be permitted" in Article 22 into "shall be permitted" to remove this worry. See Driscoll, op. cit., p. 25; and Egypt-U.S. Business Council, op. cit., p. 15.

9. See Roy, op. cit., p. 20, and Egypt-U.S. Business Council, op. cit., pp. 14–18, 31–34.

10. The best discussion of the uncertainties and ambiguities in the tax holiday provisions is given in Roy, op. cit., p. 19.

11. This conclusion comes from ibid., p. 24.

12. A major exception to equality in treatment between foreign and Egyptian firms is that

wholly Egyptian projects are not totally guaranteed against nationalization or confiscation. See ibid., p. 27 and 39.

13. Good accounts of the somewhat improved working relationships between government and business appear in Arthur D. Little, Inc., *An Assessment of Egypt's Industrial Sector,* Report to the Special Interagency Task Force Reviewing the U.S. Security Supporting Assistance Program for Egypt (Cambridge, MA, January 1978), pp. 39–42; and Driscoll, op. cit., pp. 52–53. For example, an enterprise may introduce new products for uncontrolled domestic and export markets if there is no interference with the attainment of planned output targets and if the necessary funds and materials are available.

14. As summarized in the National Foreign Trade Council's *Middle East Notes* No. 48 of October 23, 1975.

RESPONSE BY FOREIGN INVESTORS

The evolution of a vastly improved legal framework during the 1973–77 period has elicited a large number of approaches to the Egyptian government on the part of foreign investors. These initial approaches have also resulted in a fairly impressive number of project approvals. Actual implementation of projects has, however, fallen far short of initial expectations.

The statistical record of foreign projects approved and in operation is presented first, followed by an analysis of the foreign investor experience in banking and petroleum. Foreign investor plans in other sectors are then described. The second section presents information on an investment stimulation program and some of the factors that might explain the meager results achieved.

THE INVESTMENT RECORD

Large numbers of foreign investors were impressed with the marked improvement in the foreign investment climate in Egypt after the October 1973 war. The extent of their interest in exploring investment opportunities was broadened by the promulgation of the comprehensive foreign investment code of 1974, the responsive 1977 amendment and the changes in the other laws and regulations described in the previous chapter. The result was many exploratory visits to Cairo and a fair number of project approvals. By comparison, Law No. 65 of 1971 had resulted in only 46 approved projects, of which just five had reached the production stage over a two-year period.

As detailed in Table 4.1 no fewer than 744 projects have been approved over the three-and-a-half-year period, July 1974 to December 1977, with proposed foreign equity of £E1.37 billion and Egyptian equity of £E472

TABLE 4.1: Foreign Investment Project Approvals, July 1974 to December 1977 (in £E millions)

Inland Projects	Number	Approved Capital		
		Local	Foreign	Total
Investment companies	28	21,102	147,028	168,130
Banking institutions	34	32,340	79,360	111,700
Tourism	89	75,372	248,979	324,351
Housing	31	114,987	97,913	212,900
Transport	13	2,586	136,727	139,313
Health	12	7,336	21,524	28,860
Agriculture	23	34,450	39,999	74,449
Contracting	23	6,303	8,748	15,051
Education and training	1	—	2,800	2,800
Textiles	29	59,217	37,203	96,420
Food and beverages	19	4,440	5,929	10,369
Chemicals	89	31,355	71,138	102,493
Engineering	38	20,288	37,398	57,686
Building materials	19	25,482	23,628	49,110
Metallurgy	23	9,504	13,527	23,031
Pharmaceuticals	8	3,085	3,822	6,907
Mining	3	709	2,429	3,138
Total	482	448,556	978,152	1,426,708
Public free zone projects	201	17,227	208,053	225,280
Private free zone projects	61	6,690	184,875	191,571
Grand Total	744	472,479	1,371,080	1,843,550*

*Amounts exclude loan financing. Total for inland projects inclusive of loan financing would be £E1.8 billion. Grand total would be £E3.0 billion.
Source: Financial Times, July 31, 1978.

million.[1] At the end of December 1976, the cumulative number of projects was 534, with foreign and Egyptian equities of £E1.36 billion and £E268 million respectively. Particularly noteworthy is the sharp rise in the proposed Egyptian equity participation during 1977.

The cumulative figure for total approved foreign capital as of December 31, 1977, is almost identical to the corresponding figure at the end of 1976. In fact, there was a decline from the £E1.71 billion shown to be outstanding as of June 30, 1977. This decline does not primarily represent slack foreign investor interest during 1977, although the results are certainly disappointing to Egyptian officials, as explained below. Rather, there has been an effort to weed out dead projects. A project approval is granted for an initial six-month period, and a six-month extension is routinely given if investors are proceeding in a timely fashion. Subsequent extensions require the approval of the Authority. By June 30, 1977, only 25 originally approved projects had been denied requested renewals of their licenses; apparently a greater number of projects have been removed from the Authority's list during the last half of 1977, due to no action being taken to implement projects.

It will be noticed from Table 4.1 that the number of projects approved outside the free zones was 482, with a total approved capital of £E978 million. The main fields of interest are investment companies, banks, tourism, housing, transportation, agriculture, textiles, engineering, and chemicals. Since petroleum is under a special law, it should be noted that none of the investment statistics here or below include petroleum in which more than one billion dollars has been or is being invested.

When we turn to the implementation of projects, the situation is far from satisfactory. The General Authority for Investment and Free Zones has carried out surveys of approved investment projects to determine the progress of implementation. The three categories are "approved," "in execution," and "in production." "Approved" means that a government license has been granted for the project, while "in execution" indicates that investors have started to take the necessary legal and administrative steps for establishing the company. "In production" means that all necessary equipment has been imported, the factory or building constructed, and production or operations begun.[2] Under these definitions, 103 projects outside the free zones are listed in Table 4.2 as being in execution as of June 30, 1977, with a total capital of £E310 million, and a hundred projects in production, with a total capital of £E181 million. In the free zone areas, 61 projects, with a total capital of £E61 million, are in operation; most of them are storage and service projects.

The U.S. equity stake in projects actually in operation is estimated to be $129 million, of which the great bulk has gone into the banking sector. These Egyptian statistics, omitting as they do data for petroleum activities, are dwarfed by the figures from the U.S. Department of Commerce which show that U.S. petroleum investments may have been several hundred million dollars during the 1973 to 1977 period.[3]

TABLE 4.2: Inland Foreign Investment Projects Approved and Being Implemented as of June 30, 1977 (capital valued in £E millions)

	Approved		In Execution		In Production	
	Number	Total Capital	Number	Total Capital	Number	Total Capital
1. Investment companies	20	167.5	4	44.0	5	98.6
2. Banking institutions	20	74.0	6	10.8	17	40.2
3. Tourism	75	253.3	18	77.7	11	13.7
4. Housing	24	144.9	7	75.0	1	.05
5. Transportation	12	139.6	2	10.7	3	3.2
6. Health	8	36.0	2	2.4	—	—
7. Agricultural	15	27.6	3	1.3	—	—
8. Construction	20	7.5	1	0.1	7	3.5
9. Textile	26	94.0	7	16.1	10	4.0
10. Food and beverages	22	56.7	9	5.3	—	—
11. Chemical	94	117.0	21	23.2	34	14.3
12. Engineering	20	33.0	5	5.8	5	0.8
13. Building materials	14	33.5	7	25.5	2	0.9
14. Metallurgical	19	16.4	8	11.0	3	0.8
15. Pharmaceutical	5	2.9	2	0.9	—	—
16. Mining	4	2.8	1	0.6	2	0.7
Total	408	1,182.0	103	310.4	100	180.8

Source: Arthur D. Little, Inc., *An Assessment of Egypt's Industrial Sector,* Report to the Special Interagency Task Force Reviewing the U.S. Security Supporting Assistance Program for Egypt (Cambridge, MA, January 1978), p. 75.

Banking

The most important sector by far at the production or operation stage is investment companies and banking. The five investment companies account for 55 percent of the committed capital, and the seventeen banks another 22 percent. Six of the banks have been established in joint venture partnership with the state-owned banks, and the remainder as "offshore" bank branches confined under Law No. 43 to foreign currency operations. There are an additional dozen or so representative offices.

It is natural that banks and investment companies be the early foreign investor entrants since one of their main functions is to be in a good position to advise other prospective foreign investor clients on host market conditions and to act as their financial intermediaries. There has been some criticism, however, in the Egyptian press and parliament that few of the banking institutions have so far been involved in the productive sectors of the economy. Bankers have rather concentrated on financing private sector trade and the needs of the service sector. With a continuing strong rise in deposits and a perceived shortage of "good" local lending opportunities, the banks have placed substantial sums on the Eurodollar market. This situation has further embittered some critics, who have claimed that the foreign banks were draining resources from the Egyptian economy.

It must be remembered, however, that early in 1977, a Chase Manhattan Bank consortium arranged a seven-year loan of $250 million to spread out some of the Egyptian government's pressing short-term obligations. In November 1977, most of the government's issue of $200 million in development bonds was taken up by the banks. Several banks have indeed become directly involved in industrial projects. Cairo Barclays International has extended loans for twelve operating projects in such fields as paper manufacture, shoes, furniture, textiles, and aluminum extrusion. The Misr-Iran Development Bank, which was established in 1974 through an agreement between the Egyptian and Iranian governments and has since received at least $15 million in loans from the Iranian government, has extended industrial subloans in such fields as sugar, aluminum, textiles, and electronics. The pre-feasibility studies prepared by this Egyptian-Iranian bank have apparently proved effective in bringing joint venture partners together to launch detailed feasibility studies for determining whether the projects should go forward and receive the bank's loans. The pre-feasibility analysis done by other governmental or private institutions has apparently not been thorough enough for eliciting wide domestic or foreign investor interest. The Development Industrial Bank, reorganized by the government in 1976, has also played an increasing catalytic role in mobilizing industrial investment and will have received up to $100 million from the U.S. Agency for International Development through 1979 for this purpose.[4]

Private bankers have also pointed to government restrictions which have hampered their greater participation in local ventures. All banks in Egypt aside from offshore banks must place 20 percent of their reserves as non-interest bearing deposits with the central bank. Even interbank placements had to conform to this 20 percent reserve requirement. Furthermore, domestic interest rates continued lower than abroad. In April 1978, the Central Bank finally waived reserve requirements on interbank placements, thus making this activity more feasible for foreign joint venture banks. In June 1978, interest rates were raised across the board from 8–9 percent plus 38 percent commission to a competitive 9–11 percent plus 3/8 percent commission.

Another serious restriction on private banking activity is the tradition that public sector companies have recourse only to the four government-owned banks, Bank Misr, Banque du Caire, National Bank, and Bank of Alexandria. One of the beneficial side effects of the reorganization of public sector companies, under Law No. 111 of September 18, 1975, was the fact that these companies no longer had to obtain all their financing through government banks, but could go elsewhere. One joint venture bank accordingly approached cotton cooperatives with an offer of finance, but was refused in deference to the traditional government sources. Only after much contact with the Central Bank, was permission given for the private loan arrangement. In many other public sector areas, foreign bank activity is permitted, especially after a transitional period ended on July 1, 1978, but foreign bankers suspect that pressure is still being applied to public sector companies to stick with the nationally-owned banks.[5]

Petroleum

Creation of the Ministry of Petroleum in 1973 eased the foreign exchange problems of the petroleum sector. Foreign companies exploring for oil were exempt from the usual restrictions against the transfer of currency and received assistance from the Ministry in clearing the imports of needed equipment. Some 50 exploration and production agreements have been signed with 26 foreign oil companies from 1973 to 1978, including such companies as Exxon, Mobil Oil, Petrobras, Amoco, and Atlantic Richfield from which Egypt has received $92 million in signature bonuses. These production sharing agreements provide for oil company recovery of exploration costs if oil is found in commercial quantities. After this cost recovery, the remaining oil is divided, with the government taking between 65 and 87 percent, depending on the particular agreement and the circumstances. Company operations are carried out on a joint venture basis between the foreign oil company and the government agency, the Egyptian General Petroleum Corporation.[6]

Other Sectors

Leaving aside the banking and petroleum sectors, the total capital committed to projects in operation is only £E42 million. As shown in Table 4.2, tourism and chemicals account for two-thirds of this investment. The bulk of investments is not being made in capital-intensive activities, but rather in areas promising quick returns such as trading and service activities and consumer products.

In any case, the statistics on capital approvals outside the banking and petroleum sectors give a not very good impression of the foreign investment activity which has been going on. Much descriptive information on foreign investor intentions in Egypt has appeared in brief articles over the last four years in such general newspapers as the *Financial Times* and the *Journal of Commerce,* and such Middle Eastern publications as *MidEast Report, Mid-East Markets,* and *Middle East Newsletter.* I have prepared digests of these articles on a monthly basis, and, while the information is necessarily random and sketchy and may not cover a majority of the important transactions taking place, brief excerpts are provided below to give the reader a better idea of the foreign investor involvement outside banking and petroleum.[7]

Tourism has attracted much attention. An agreement was reached in the summer of 1974 between Egyptian partners and Holiday Inns on a $4 million, 200-room hotel near Cairo International Airport. During the same year, Sheraton officials announced plans to establish Sheraton hotels in Cairo, Alexandria, and Luxor. In early 1975, a new 702-room Marriott hotel was announced for Cairo. Eximbank and Bank of America loans of $3.9 million each were to assist the $38 million hotel. A new $50 million 850-room Semiramis Hotel in Cairo was planned by Saudi-Egyptian interests in 1975. During the summer of 1976, French, Egyptian, Iranian, and Gulf companies signed a $37 million agreement to construct a 500-room hotel on Gezira Island. The Misr-Iran-France Hotel Company is investing 70 percent of the hotel's $12.5 million capital, and a French company, Jacques Borel International, is to act as the manager. Late in 1976, an agreement was reached with Holiday Inns to manage a $40 million, 1,000-bed hotel near Cairo being built by a consortium of Italian firms and largely owned by the government or government-controlled concerns. The Arab International Company for Hotels and Tourism announced, early in 1977, plans for a $60 million Ramses Hilton Hotel in Cairo to be built by a Swiss firm. Triad, an American-Saudi joint venture, is linking up with an Egyptian firm, El Shams, to build a $56 million complex near El Montazah, consisting of a 350-room hotel and 400 apartments. The two partners are also planning a $14 million office building in downtown Cairo. Ramada International has agreed to manage the 500-room Ramada Nile-Cairo under construction in Gizah. In October 1978, two Finnish firms won a $12 million contract to build a Holiday Inn in the same town with 156 rooms. By far the largest tourist project was the $500 million residential and resort complex planned near the pyramids in Gizah by the Southern Pacific Property of Hong Kong and the Egyptian Tourism Development Company. This complex would have consisted of five hotels, 5,800 villas, and 5,100 apartments, but was canceled abruptly by the Egyptian government in the summer of 1978 for environmental reasons.

There are no convenient divisions for foreign investment activity outside banking, petroleum, and tourism. Consequently, the following descriptions of the other activities will be lumped together in rough chronological order.

1974

Brazilian, Japanese, and German interests were to contribute 50 percent of the equity and the Egyptian government another 50 percent in a $130 million reduced-iron plant near Alexandria. The Midrex process was to be used and the annual output was scheduled to be 1.6 million tons.

A 7-Up bottling plant was announced with an annual output of three million cases. The investment involved might be $8 million.

John J. McMullen Associates joined with the General Organization for the Maritime Transport of Alexandria on a 40 to 60 percent basis to establish the Egyptian Overseas Maritime Transport Company.

1975

Two German companies established a $90 million fertilizer plant near Alexandria for the production of 1,000 tons of nitrate urea fertilizer per year.

The governments of Saudi Arabia, the United Arab Emirates, and Qatar joined the Egyptian government in establishing in Cairo the Arab Organization for Industrialization, capitalized at $1 billion. Both military and civilian equipment were to be included. This venture was very long-term, but was reminiscient of Mohammed Ali's efforts in the 1820s to establish military industries.

Bechton Dickinson International (French) established a $10 million company in Port Said to produce 100 million plastic syringes annually.

The Arizona Colorado Land & Livestock Raising Company joined Egyptian companies in a $33 million project to raise 3,000 milch cows and produce 20 million liters of milk annually as well as substantial quantities of cheese, yogurt, and beef. The reclamation of 16,000 acres of adjacent land would also take place. The American company would own 49 percent of the project's equity and the Egyptian companies the remainder.

1976

I-T-E World Trade Corporation was setting up a technical services headquarters in Alexandria to direct the sales of its transmission and hydraulic equipment throughout the middle East.

The Egyptian government had long tried to complete negotiations with Union Carbide on the erection of a 150,000 ton-per-year ethylene plant and with Amoco on an 80,000 ton-per-year, $75 million DMT plant, but without success.

Hoescht Orient established a $4 million pharmaceutical plant in Cairo which was expected to produce about $14 million worth of products annually. The plant was owned 60–40 percent by Hoescht and the Egyptian government. Pfizer and Swisspharma had already entered the Egyptian market under similar arrangements. Total sales of all pharmaceuticals during 1974 by all companies were approximately £E40 million.

A French company supplied technical assistance and one-half of the equity to establish a $15 million factory in Ismailia for color TV sets and electronic components. The initial production was scheduled to be 5,000 sets annually.

Plans for a new Schindler elevator plant were announced. The capacity of the Otis Elevator plant had recently been expanded from 40 to 100 yearly.

Michelin was setting up a $60 million plant in Alexandria for the production of tires for heavy trucks. The French company was to own 60 percent of the plant's equity and the Egyptian government the remainder.

The construction of the McEvoy oil well head equipment plant near Cairo had recently been completed.

The Arab Aluminum Company constructed a $10 million aluminum fabricating plant in Ismailia for the production of building materials, truck bodies, and irrigation pipes. The raw materials were derived from the nearby Nag Hammadi aluminum smelter. The Citibank branch in Cairo provided a loan of $2.9 million for the project, and the American University of Cairo's Educational Endowment Fund $2.5 million. The remaining funds were obtained from American, Arab, and Egyptian investors. The plant opened in October 1977 with an initial production rate of 2,000 tons annually, some of which was for export to Saudi Arabia and the Gulf. A $50 million expansion in production to 8,000 tons annually was planned.

The Arab Ceramic Company was building a $19 million ceramic plant in Abu Zaabal near Cairo. The International Finance Corporation invested $750,000 in equity, and extended a $4,250,000 loan for the project. The Bank of Alexandria extended loans of $5 million and Egyptian insurance companies $2 million. The government-owned General Company for Ceramics & Porcelain was to hold 30 percent of the equity, other Egyptian investors 25 percent, the Saudi Singab Company for Trading & Industry 15 percent, and Kuwaiti investors 20 percent. The plant was expected to produce 5,000 tons of vitreous sanitary ware and 12,000 tons of ceramic wall tile annually.

West European and Arab interests established the Bavarian Food Corporation on a 55–45 percent basis. The $69 million company was expected to produce 25,000 tons of baby food, 300,000 tons of milk and yogurt, and

600,000 hectoliters of soft drinks annually. A brewery with an annual production of 40,000 tons of malt and one million hectoliters of beer was to be added.

Polyester Fibers of Egypt, Ltd., a joint venture of the Fahmy Trading Company of New York and Arab investors, was to build a $124 million polyester fiber plant near Alexandria. Fahmy was to hold 40 percent of the equity. The plant was to have a 25,000-ton annual capacity, and two spinning mills were to be constructed for blended yarn.

1977

(Perhaps corroborating the Egyptian sense of disappointment at the lack óf serious foreign investor interest is the fact that the previous news item was dated June 1976, while the following item is dated July 1977. No significant plan of foreign investor participation in Egypt outside the banking, petroleum, and tourism sectors was reported in the general or regional publications in the interim.)

The Inter-Arab Investment Guarantee Corporation issued a $7 million investment guarantee on a Lebanese-Egyptian venture. The guarantee covered the equity of the Lebanese partner, who is supplying 75 percent of the capital cost of the $9 million sanitary ware factory. The initial annual output was 5,000 tons, with a doubling in production expected within two years.

Coca-Cola signed a joint venture agreement with five Egyptian entities on a 50–50 percent basis to develop a $10 million agricultural venture near Ismailia. Citrus groves were to be developed over about 15,000 acres. Coca-Cola hoped that the agreement would lead the Egyptian government to remove its name from the Arab boycott list. Coca-Cola had been forced out of Egypt in 1967 because of the boycott, and a local imitator, Si-Cola, had taken over the former Coca-Cola plant. Pepsi Cola had been bottled in Egypt for twenty years, while Canada Dry and 7-Up were recent entries. The annual production of Si-Cola and Pepsi in government-owned plants during 1977 was 27 and 17 million cases respectively; these amounts were expected to double by 1984. Canada Dry and 7-Up were produced by the newly founded Cairo Beverages, a privately owned company of Egyptian and foreign investors. Production in 1978 was about 7 million cases and was expected to rise to about 13 million cases in 1979.[8]

The Ford Motor Company reached an agreement with the government on construction of a $145 million factory to produce 10,000 trucks and 50,000 diesel engines yearly by 1985. Ford Motor subscribed 30 percent of the $30 million equity, the Egyptian government 40 percent, and other Arab investors the remaining 30 percent. The components were to be almost exclusively British in the beginning, while the local content was to rise gradually to 40 percent by 1985. Most of the sales were planned for other Arab countries. The agreement would go into effect upon removal of Ford from the Arab boycott list; at that time, the former Ford automobile assembly plant at Alexandria would also be able to resume production after plant rehabilitation.

Thomson-Brandt (France) made a $30 million investment with Ideal Company of Egypt to boost its annual output of refrigerators from 130,000 to 250,000. A new washing machine unit was to become operational at the plant and would increase production to 150,000 washing machines a year.

American Motors Corporation formed a joint venture with the Arab Organization for Industrialization to produce utility vehicles. AMC was to own 49 percent of the shares of the venture and the governmental organization the remainder. The 200,000 square foot plant was to have an annual production capacity of 11,000 vehicles.

Reynolds International of the United States and Arab Contractors of Egypt formed a joint venture, called Alumisr, to build an aluminum extrusion plant at Helwan. Reynolds took 12.5 percent of the shares and provided management services for the construction and operation of the plant. Arab Contractors took 20 percent of the shares, and several Egyptian banks the remainder of the $6 million capital. Alumisr planned an annual production of 4,000 tons of pipes, door frames, windows, wheels, and industrial bars. (The previous four items were all announced during October, thus indicating a certain peak of foreign investor interest. The opening of the Arab Aluminum Company plant, begun during 1976, see above, also took place during the same month.)

Mainzeal Corporation of New Zealand joined with Misr Foreign Trade Company on a 50–50 percent basis to build a $14 million plant for cheese and reconstituted milk.

A $75 million agreement was signed between British Aerospace Dynamics Group and the Arab Organization for Industrialization to set up a plant near Cairo to manufacture antitank guided missiles. Some components will be exported from the United Kingdom with an increasing percentage to be made in Egypt. A joint company, Arab-British Dynamics, was formed to manage the plant.

1978

The first Massey-Ferguson plant in Cairo was able to assemble 2,000 tractors per year. A $50 million contract was approved for another plant near Alexandria to produce 5,000 tractors per year as well as other farm tools and Perkins diesel engines. The new plant was to obtain 25 percent of its components locally when it begins production in 1981, with the local content rising to 72 percent within six years. Massey-Ferguson was to hold 30 percent of the equity, a Saudi company 20 percent, and Egyptian interests 50 percent.

Kloeckner-Humbolt-Deutz of West Germany was building a plant at

Ismailia under a $45 million contract and was to hold 25.1 percent of the capital. The plant was to produce tractors, diesel motors, and generating and pumping units.

The Egyptian American Insurance Company, a joint venture between American International Underwriters Overseas Ltd. and Al Chark, opened. The new company was to handle all types of insurance, except life insurance, for U.S. and international companies with initial concentration on marine cargo coverages.

Cairo Beverage & Industrial Company was formed to produce 7-Up and Canada Dry beverages. The $15.2 million capital was supplied by investors from Egypt, Oman, Yemen, Saudi Arabia, and the United States.

Fiat (Italy) and Seat (Spain) formed a $32 million joint venture with El-Nasr Automotive Manufacturing Company and the Misr-Iran Development Bank to increase production at the El-Nasr assembly plant near Cairo. Fiat held 20 percent of the shares, Seat 10, El-Nasr 43, and Misr-Iran 27 percent. The annual production capacity was expected to increase by 23,000 cars to 35,000 by 1981.

The International Finance Corporation agreed to invest $23 million in a $126 million sugar project. The project was carried out by the Delta Sugar Company, with $34.2 million in equity from Egyptian companies, $4.7 million from Fives-Cail-Babcock of France, the supplier of sugar mill equipment for the project, and $6.2 million from the Islamic Development Bank. The company planned to reclaim 48,000 acres of saline soil in the northern Delta and to raise sugar beets. It planned to process its own sugar beets and those to be purchased from other Egyptian producers. The project aimed to produce 100,000 tons of sugar per year.

Anagood was formed to reclaim 23,100 acres at Wadi Karkar, south of Aswan. The new company was capitalized at $10 million, with 40 percent coming from American agribusiness firms, 35 percent from the Ministry of Reconstruction, and 25 percent from the Egyptian public.

A $15 million razor blade plant was inaugurated on November 6 in Alexandria. The annual production capacity was scheduled to be 200 million blades. The plant was a joint venture of the Egyptian government and Wilkinson Sword Company of London.

Saxon Industries announced a joint venture with an Egyptian distribution company to establish a photocopier facility in Alexandria. Photocopiers will be manufactured there for distribution throughout the Middle East.

Mann & Hummel of West Germany joined with four Egyptian investors in a $66 million project to manufacture motor filters.

Confinanz of Switzerland became a participant in a $2.3 million project to make blankets and velour cloth.

Another major indicator of the attractiveness of the investment climate is the behavior of Egyptian investors. This behavior is presented in Tables 4.3

TABLE 4.3: Domestic Investment Approvals, 1970–76 (£E thousands)

Year	Number of Projects	Investment (planned)	Annual Value of Production	Annual Net Value Added	Employment	Wages
1970	314	5,000	10,800	2,300	5,635	775
1971	280	6,900	12,500	2,500	4,944	855
1972	350	8,600	16,500	2,600	6,308	1,035
1973	332	16,700	19,700	4,600	10,546	1,693
1974	358	19,100	28,700	4,300	8,589	1,732
1975	740	67,100	132,300	40,000	17,231	5,100
1976	693	94,773	213,297	53,811	20,655	6,805

Source: Little, op. cit., p. 77.

and 4.4, where a marked acceleration in interest is noted after 1973 and 1974. Whereas, 332 domestic investments were approved in 1973, with a total investment of £E16.7 million, these figures jumped to 693 and £E94.8 million by 1976. As with foreign investors, chemicals proved the most attractive outlet for Egyptian investors, with textiles, engineering, and food also important. The amount of actual investments undertaken in connection with these approved domestic projects is unknown, but is presumed not to exceed one-third of the approved amounts.[9]

TABLE 4.4: Domestic Investment Approvals by Sector, 1973 and 1975

	Number of Licenses		Total Investment (£E thousands)		Employment Number
	1973	1975	1973	1975	1975
Engineering	181	197	9,895	10,818	3,246
Textiles	30	181	1,272	12,238	4,468
Chemicals	44	143	1,259	17,540	3,363
Food	27	127	835	10,177	2,018
Leather	24	31	1,616	7,100	1,729
Electrical	14	29	744	7,165	1,603
Metallurgical	11	20	935	1,389	530
Mining	1	12	128	1,698	274
Total	332	740	16,684	67,124	17,231

Source: Delwin A. Roy, *Private Industry Sector Development in Egypt: An Analysis of Trends, 1973–77*, Report to the Special Interagency Task Force Reviewing the U.S. Security Supporting Assistance Program for Egypt (Washington, D.C.: Agency for International Development, January 1978), p. 11.

A picture of investments in the public industrial sector is given in Table 4.5. The same pattern of accelerating involvement is revealed, with total investments rising from £E87 million in 1973 to £E213 million in 1976. Here the development in chemicals is less significant than developments in the other industrial sectors.

REASONS FOR SLOW IMPLEMENTATION DESPITE STIMULATION PROGRAM

In addition to the many individual foreign investors who have made initial contacts with Egyptian government authorities, there has also been an organized investment stimulation program. Despite all these initial contacts

TABLE 4.5: Investments in the Public Industrial Sector, 1973–76 (£E millions, current prices)

Subsector	1973	1974	1975	1976
Textiles	30.4	35.2	47.4	81.4
Domestic	16.9	16.5	27.2	37.3
Foreign	13.5	18.7	20.2	44.1
Foodstuffs	13.8	24.4	38.1	42.7
Domestic	11.0	13.0	21.8	26.3
Foreign	2.8	11.4	16.3	16.4
Chemicals	22.5	28.4	35.4	36.2
Domestic	17.3	21.7	20.6	22.0
Foreign	5.2	6.7	14.8	14.2
Engineering and metallurgical	20.3	18.0	31.3	49.5
Domestic	16.0	13.4	23.5	37.4
Foreign	4.3	4.6	7.8	12.1
Mining	0.5	1.0	2.6	2.9
Domestic	0.5	0.5	1.7	2.4
Foreign	—	0.5	0.9	0.5
Total	87.5	107.0	154.8	212.7
Domestic	61.7	65.1	94.8	125.4
Foreign	25.8	41.9	60.0	87.3

Source: Little, op. cit., p. 29.

and the investment program, the follow-through was meager for a number of reasons, both external to Egypt and related to a number of Egyptian environmental factors.

During the inaugural meeting of the Egypt-U.S. Business Council in Cairo on October 12–14, 1975, a Development Projects Review Team was established. This team sifted through 265 projects which Egyptian officials considered worthy of implementation, and, by April 1976, had winnowed down the list to 35 projects. Within the next few months, the list was further refined to number 24 projects chosen for a hard-sell investment stimulation program.

David Scott, Chairman of Allis-Chalmers and former Chairman of the U.S. section of the Egypt-U.S. Business Council, seconded the nomination of Lucien Bruggeman from Allis-Chalmers to serve for nine months until July 31, 1977, at the Egyptian Economic Mission in New York as "investment development officer." James Potts, a retired Union Carbide executive, agreed to serve in a liaison capacity in Cairo for a six-month period.[10] David Scott wrote to his counterparts at other companies concerning the 24 promising projects, and Lucien Bruggeman followed through with 68 detailed presentations to company presidents and vice presidents, making use of the brief pre-feasibility studies prepared by the Council regarding these projects. Twenty of the companies contacted were sufficiently interested to send teams to Egypt for further studies and contacts, but only a few appeared to maintain continuing tentative interest. Almost all the companies contacted by Arnold McKay in March 1978 denied that they had a definite interest in the projects they had explored, being no more than "interested in principle."[11]

The program of the U.S. Agency for International Development in Cairo is also stimulating American investors to make initial contacts. Since fiscal year 1975, AID has financed 30 feasibility studies, costing in the range of about $45,000 each, and apparently stands ready, on a highly selective basis, to make loans to joint venture projects, either directly or through the Development Industrial Bank or other banking institutions.

When explanations are sought for the relatively slow pace of implementation of foreign investment projects in Egypt and for the continuing paucity of foreign investment proposals, a distinction should be made between the legal and environmental aspects. As noted in the last chapter, the Egyptian government has made enormous strides in removing many impediments in the legal and regulatory framework so that the remaining legal problems do not constitute a very serious obstacle to foreign investor interest. On the other hand, the environmental problems are more difficult to handle, and much more time is needed for their resolution or at least substantial improvement. These problems are discussed in Chapter 6 and, in order of descending priority, are represented by the regional situation of war or peace; relationships with the government; infrastructural facilities; capital and foreign exchange availabilities and skills.

There are several other explanations for the slow movement of foreign investment, and they have little to do with the situation in Egypt. First is the general recession in the world economy, which started in late 1973 and coincided with Egypt's newly adopted Open Door policy. Since then, foreign investors have been more cautious in entering all host countries. This greater aversion to risks has made many investors adopt a "wait-and-see" attitude, emphasizing the remaining negative aspects of foreign investment climates rather than the positive aspects.

Arnold McKay points to competitive considerations as being a possible factor behind the pattern of foreign investment. One observer he contacted believes that some multinationals are worried that competitors may get established in Egypt and thereby benefit from favorable tariffs. These multinationals obtain approval for their ventures and then just sit on the approvals. They can move quickly if their competitors also move.[12] Other observers say that some Egyptian officials prefer to deal with the very largest firms and create difficulties for the smaller firms. If the projected deal turns sour, the official can always say, "But I took the biggest and the best."

Perhaps the most apt comment about the overall situation is Roy's: "There has been no 'landslide' of private investment, and, given the recent history of Egypt, there most probably never could have been. Expectations in this regard on the part of the government and the private sector have been inflated and occasionally naive."[13] The time since the turnaround in the Egyptian investment climate has been short, and substantial foreign investor interest can still be anticipated over a longer period.

NOTES

1. The table is obtained from *Financial Times* (July 31, 1978). An analysis of the final 1976 figures is given in "Progress Report Regarding Open-Door Policy Projects in Egypt as at the End of 1976," National Bank of Egypt, *Economic Bulletin* (No. 2, 1977), pp. 152–61.

2. See Arthur D. Little Inc., *An Assessment of Egypt's Industrial Sector,* Report to the Special Interagency Task Force Reviewing the U.S. Security Supporting Assistance Program for Egypt (Cambridge: MA, January, 1978), p. 74, for a description of these three clarifications and of the approval process generally.

3. See Arnold McKay, "U.S. Investors Fail To Rush Into Egypt," *Journal of Commerce* (March 27, 1978).

4. Delwin A. Roy, *Private Industry Sector Development in Egypt: An Analysis of Trends, 1973–1977,* Report to the Special Interagency Task Force Reviewing the U.S. Security Supporting Assistance Program for Egypt (Washington, D.C.: USAID, January, 1978), pp. 31–34, and "Foreign Banks Move In," *Financial Times* (July 31, 1978) have some interesting comments on the present and prospective role of the various banks in venture capital operations and industrial development. See also, Little, op. cit., p. 123, on the need for more pre-feasibility analyses for attracting more investment. For information on AID's support of the Development Industrial Bank, see Agency for International Development, *U.S. Economic Assistance to Egypt, A Report of a Special Interagency Task Force* (Washington, D.C.: February 1978, pp. 20, 21, 27, 28).

5. An excellent account of the environment for foreign bank activity in Egypt is given in "Foreign Banks Move In," op. cit., pp. 14–15.

6. The production sharing agreements are briefly described in "Steady Income from Oil," *Financial Times* (July 31, 1978), p. 17.

7. These digests, titled *Middle East & North African Notes,* have appeared as monthly publications of the National Foreign Trade Council.

8. The additional source used here is "Egypt, An Oasis for Soft Drinks," *New York Times* (August 1, 1978).

9. See Little, op. cit., pp. 76–77.

10. The trials and tribulations of the Egyptian investment stimulation program run by American business executives are well described in McKay, "Program to Stir U.S. Investment in Egypt Generally in Limbo," *Journal of Commerce* (March 28, 1978).

11. Ibid. The investment program was scheduled to run for three years, but with the expiration of the assignments of Potts and Bruggeman in April and July 1977 respectively and the failure to appoint any replacements, the program appeared to have lapsed.

12. See McKay, "U.S. Investment in Egypt May Grow," *Journal of Commerce* (March 29, 1978). Other studies also confirm the "bandwagon" entry of rival foreign investors in accord with the Behrman direct investment model. That is, in a certain product line in a given host country, no entries of foreign investors take place for a long time. Then numerous entries take place over a short period. See, for example, David W. Carr, *Foreign Investment and Development in the Southwest Pacific with Special Reference to Australia and Indonesia,* (New York: Praeger Special Studies, 1978) pp. 98–99.

13. See Roy, op. cit., p. 35.

5

RECENT ECONOMIC
PROGRESS

Egypt's general economy started to grow strongly during 1975 and may now be on a sustained high-growth path. Whereas the real rate of increase in the gross domestic product averaged only 2.6 percent per year from 1965 to 1973 and was 3.2 percent during 1974, there was a spurt to 9.8 percent during 1975. The growth rate was 7.4 percent during 1976 and 8.3 percent during 1977. The average rate of growth experienced in the Egyptian economy during 1975–77 of over 8 percent annually is even higher than the 6.7 percent annual average experienced from 1956 to 1965.

The open-door policy of the Egyptian government toward foreign and domestic investors and the ensuing revival of private enterprise activity can certainly take much credit for this acceleration in growth. The other significant factors underlying this growth acceleration was the reopening of the Suez Canal, the growth in tourism, the surge in emigrant remittances, the rise in petroleum activity, and substantial foreign assistance. Industrial output has also been increasing steadily, and some diversification has been achieved.

SOME NONINDUSTRIAL SECTORS GROWING SPECTACULARLY

Before turning to those nonindustrial sectors that have been making major strides in recent years and have contributed to the vitality of the entire economy, I will briefly describe two economic problems holding back rapid progress. These are military expenditures and the population/agriculture ratio.

As a result of four Arab-Israeli wars and other frequent turbulence in the Middle East during the last three decades, military expenditures have skyrocketed. As a percentage of the gross domestic product, military spending was

6 percent during the late 1950s, 11 percent during the first half of the 1960s, 20 percent from 1967 to 1974, and perhaps 25 percent in recent years.[1] Since military spending is highly import-intensive in Egypt, and, in all countries, diverts resources from more productive uses, this very high rate of military expenditure has acted as a significant drag on the overall economy.

Egypt's current population problem is of recent origin. In 1800, the country had only four million people, the lowest in recent history and probably only half the ancient number. Plagues and wars kept the number down to five million until 1850, and, by 1900, the population had risen gradually to ten million.[2] The population increase rate was still moderate from 1900 to 1940, perhaps averaging about 1.3 percent per year. There was some acceleration during the 1940s to perhaps 1.8 percent, and then the rate became a disturbing 2.5 percent during the 1950s.[3] The current rate of increase is about 2.3 percent, and the population has grown to forty million, or four times the number at the turn of the century. Since the great bulk of the land area of Egypt is desert, the size of the population now and in prospect over the next few years represents a tremendous burden on the productive resources of the economy.

One way the population burden manifests itself is in the high proportion of national income spent on consumption. Until 1975, this proportion hovered consistently around 87 percent. The government has devoted a substantial part of its budget to cost-of-living subsidies to lessen the impact of inflation on the poorer citizens. At the suggestion of donor government advisors, an attempt was made in January 1977 to greatly reduce the subsidies, but the attempt was abandoned after the subsequent rioting. The annual cost of these subsidies has remained at about $1.5 billion.

The problem with Egyptian agriculture is that a revolution there had already taken place by 1912. Egypt's cultivated area had risen rapidly until 1912, but only slowly thereafter. Counting the conversion from basin to perennial irrigation, the crop area rose from 7.7 million feddans in 1912 to 8.5 million in 1938 to 10.3 million in 1958 and only to about eleven million currently.[4] The hundreds of millions of dollars spent on the Aswan High Dam promised to put an additional one million feddans of land under irrigation, but meanwhile much agricultural land has been lost to urban and industrial development. The net addition during the last twenty years or so of the dam's construction and functioning is only about 500,000 acres. The fertile area per capita fell by one-third between 1907 and 1952, and the decline since then has been even sharper, at about 40 percent. During the current 1978–82 Five-Year Plan, the government hopes to bring under cultivation or initiate a reclamation program for an additional 580,000 acres of land in an attempt to arrest this trend. A maximum of an additional 1½ million acres might be made available over the following twenty years.

Crop yields are already very high through the use of advanced technology and the intensive consumption of fertilizer. The use of fertilizer increased fourfold from 1947 to 1967. According to United Nations surveys, the output per acre in Egypt was the highest in the world for chick peas, lentils, and millet, third for rice, fifth for cotton (30 percent above U.S.), twelfth for maize, and fourteenth for wheat.[5] Crop yields are already so high that there is little room for improvement beyond their recent peak. Efforts are being made to prevent a further slippage caused by a deterioration in soil fertility and increased salinity. Drainage facilities are being improved to tackle this problem, and the World Bank, for example, is funding projects to install drains over one million acres by the end of 1979.

Some agricultural diversification has taken place. For example, the acreage devoted to the growing of fruit increased from 94 to 244 thousand acres from 1952 to 1970 and for vegetables from 261 to 717 thousand acres. A Food and Agriculture Organization study estimates that milk production could be increased by 160,000 tons per year with much greater mechanization.[6] But the significance to the overall economy of further diversification in agriculture is likewise small. Egypt must content itself in agriculture to largely standing still, even with massive domestic investments and vigorous foreign business participation in agricultural ventures.[7]

The Reopening of the Suez Canal

The dramatic economic event of 1975 was, of course, the reopening of the Suez Canal on June 5, eight years after the 1967 war had forced its closure. The report of the United Nations Conference on Trade and Development, held on October 16, 1973, estimated that the loss to the world sustained as a result of the canal's closure was at an annual rate of about $1.7 billion.[8] The loss to Egypt in canal tolls was some $200 million annually.

The new tolls were set at nearly double the previous ones and were arrived at after international consulting studies of world shipping conditions. The new rates were Special Drawing Rights (SDR) 1.611 per ton for oil, 1.722 for other cargo, and 1.289 for vessels in ballast. During the remainder of 1975 and until the middle of 1977, the numbers of ships using the canal steadily increased until leveling off at the rate of about sixty per day, or about the same as before 1967. The tonnage is doubled because of the increase in the average size of ships. A significant change is that oil tankers account for only 40 percent of the traffic compared to 75 percent before. The building of many large tankers over the last few years and the continued slump in the tanker market has made it more economical for some large tankers to go around the Cape of Good Hope, and the very large ones have to do so since they can not fit in the canal.[9] As is shown in Table 5.1, the proportion of tankers to overall shipping rose during 1976 but leveled off during 1977.

A surge in container shipping occurred during 1978. Container ships

TABLE 5.1: Some Major Economic Indicators, 1971–77

	Unit	1971	1972	1973	1974	1975	1976	1977
Crude oil production*	m. metric tons	21.0	16.0	13.5	12.2	15.8	16.7	20.9
Emigrant remittances	£E million	121	128	254	405	421	575	1,070
Tourists	,000	428	541	535	680	793	984	1,005
Ships transitting		—	—	—	—	5,579	16,806	19,703
Suez Canal tonnage		—	—	—	—	50	188	220
Tankers transitting		—	—	—	—	693	2,610	2,619
Suez Canal tonnage		—	—	—	—	14	78	76

*Includes oil from Sinai oil fields throughout. Egypt recovered their use at the end of 1975.
Sources: Data through 1976 extracted from National Bank of Egypt, *Economic Bulletin* (No. 1, 1977), pp. 50–51. The 1977 data were obtained from articles in the *Financial Times* (July 31, 1978) and from National Bank of Egypt, *Economic Bulletin* (No. 1, 1978), pp. 45–46.

had been reluctant to use the canal before 1977, owing to the high percent surcharge imposed on them. In January 1977, the Suez Canal Authority consented to halving this surcharge, and, by June, an agreement was reached between the Authority and container owners to pay a 7½ percent surcharge on the container vessels with four tiers.[10]

In 1966, the last year of operation before the closure, earnings from the Suez Canal totaled £E95 million. During 1976, earnings were £E195 million and rose to £E209 million during 1977. The dramatic impact of the opening and utilization of the Suez Canal on the overall economy is indicated by the gross domestic product figures for 1975 and 1976. The sector "transport and communications" grew by 33 percent during 1975 in constant prices, or some £E55 million. Assuming that the Suez Canal element accounted for almost all the increase, the 9.8 percent expansion in the GDP (Gross Domestic Product) during 1975 derived some 1½ percentage points from the renewed operation of the Suez Canal. The 1976 GDP figures show a 47 percent rise in the "transport and communications" sector, or £E115 million. Under the same assumption and calculations as before, the first full year's operation of the Suez Canal may have been responsible for as much as 2½ percentage points of the 7.4 percent growth which took place during 1976.[11]

Utilization of the Suez Canal has recently leveled off, but two events during the next several years should spark much greater use. Saudi Arabia is building a pipeline from its prolific oil fields near Dhahran to the Red Sea coast. Completion of this pipeline during the early 1980s would lead to greater use of the canal by tankers with Saudi crude oil. Secondly, a major widening and deepening of the 173-kilometer canal is now taking place. At the present time, vessels of up to 60,000 tons fully loaded and 250,000 tons in ballast are able to transit the canal. The World Bank is lending $100 million, Japan $222 million, the Saudi Fund for Development $50 million, USAID $25 million, other Arab financial institutions $93 million, West European governments $22 million, and the Suez Canal authority $95 million to finance major works of dredging, excavating, and building breakwaters and new bypass canal sections. Upon completion of these works by 1981, the draft of the canal will be increased from 38 to 53 feet, and the canal will then be able to accomodate ships of up to 150,000 dwt, fully loaded.[12] With these two events occurring, Suez Canal revenues could well triple to $1.2 billion annually by 1985 and may become again a major growth stimulant, making the economy attractive for greater private business participation.

Earnings from Tourism and Emigrants

The more stable climate since 1973 has caused a rise in the number of tourists. As shown in Table 5.1, they have risen steadily from 535,000 in 1973 to slightly over one million in 1977. Local spending by tourists was about

£E254 million in 1977, compared to £E189 million in 1975.[13] As noted in the last chapter, the tourist sector has absorbed a great deal of foreign investment, and the continuing high occupancy rates are attracting additional investment. Hotel capacity is expected to rise by 50,000 beds from 1978 to 1982, by which time up to 1.7 million tourists may be visiting Egypt annually.

Remittances from emigrants have become the biggest single source of foreign exchange earnings from Egypt. The rise in petroleum income after 1973 in the Gulf region and Libya attracted many skilled Egyptians to emigrate there. While the loss of many technicians and managers may have handicapped Egyptian industrial development in some areas, the share of the enhanced income returning to Egypt has been a boon to the balance of payments. The 85 percent jump in emigrant remittances during 1977, to some $1.5 billion, was particularly startling, and the World Bank estimates that these remittances could soar to $4 billion by 1986.[14]

Petroleum

Petroleum is the one sector of the economy where activity has been steady both before and after 1973. The major reason for the continuous activity is that the relations between the Egyptian government and foreign petroleum companies have been consistently harmonious and flexible throughout the 1960s and 1970s. These good relations, unlike the situation in almost all other fields, where foreign investment was discouraged during the 1960s, led to an active petroleum exploration and development program.

The fields discovered so far are small, and the average cost of production is a high $1.44 per barrel. The annual production of crude oil had reached about sixteen million tons in 1967, when the June War led to the loss of the Abu Rudeis oil fields in the Sinai. Increased production in the Morgan fields in the Gulf of Suez had restored annual production to sixteen million tons by 1971, when technical difficulties at Morgan caused production to drop to eight million tons by 1974. Water injection to bring up the pressure at Morgan, development of the offshore July and Ramadan fields and two smaller western desert fields, and the return of Abu Rudeis brought production up to twelve million tons during the next year. During 1976, production rose to seventeen million tons; by 1977, twenty-one million tons; and by 1978, twenty-six million tons.[15] The annual production is scheduled to go on rising to nearly fifty million tons by 1982.

The production of natural gas in commercial quantities began in 1975, with an output of 40,000 tons at Abu Mahdi in the Nile Delta; it rose to 130,000 tons during 1976, 400,000 tons during 1977, and 800,000 tons in 1978. The expansion of the Abu Gharadeq and Abu Kir fields should bring the annual production up to 2.7 million tons by 1982.

These significant increases in production are being promoted by strong investment commitments. Total investment funds expended in the petroleum sector went up by 79 percent during 1976 to £E47 million and jumped again to £E102 million in 1977. Of the latter figure, £E70 million was foreign investment and £E32 million domestic.[16] During the next three years, Egypt's 1978–82 Plan anticipates that petroleum investments will total some £E680 million.

The increase in petroleum production during 1976 was significant in that Egypt became a small net exporter of oil, with a surplus of £E122 million compared to a deficit of £E25 million in 1975. Petroleum exports rose by 102 percent to £E252 million, and petroleum imports fell by 13 percent to £E130 million. With the completion during that same year of the repairs to the bombed-out Suez refinery, the output of refined products at the six publicly owned refineries rose by 14 percent to 10.5 million tons. The recent additions caused the production capacity of the refineries to rise to seventeen million tons by the end of 1978.

There have been many proposals for the establishment of petrochemical industries, but no specific plans have yet been agreed on. A significant diversification in petroleum was the completion of the twin Sumed pipelines during 1976 and 1977 at an approximate cost of $500 million. The 320-kilometer line runs from Ain Sokna near Suez on the Red Sea to Sidi Kreir near Alexandria on the Mediterranean. The twin lines have a total throughput capacity of 117 million tons per year, and tankers of up to 250,000 tons can be accommodated at each end. But the lines have been running at less than 50 percent capacity and have thus been unprofitable so far. In an effort to encourage some users to expand their yearly use of the pipeline, the government in December 1977 replaced the basic transit fee of $1.60 per ton with a sliding-scale tariff. The new rates start at $1.52 per ton, moving gradually down to $1 per ton for volumes of over 14 million tons per year. The situation will be vastly improved for the lines when tanker rates rise and with completion of the Saudi Arabian oil pipeline from Dammam to the Red Sea.

Foreign Assistance

Generous assistance by foreign governments and international organizations since 1973 has been an important driving force behind the recent growth surge. The total aid from 1974 to 1977 has come to over $12 billion. Egyptians have succeeded in convincing the other Arab governments that Egypt's action in October 1973 was a serious sacrifice for the general Arab cause; on the other hand, the indirect effect was a fourfold boost in the petroleum income of the Gulf states. Grants from the other Arab states shot up to $1.3 billion during 1974, and were $988 and $635 million in 1975 and 1976 respectively. A $1.5 billion loan was provided in April 1977 for payment to Egypt that year and during 1978. Other loans, guarantees, and bank deposits by Arab governments may have totaled $2 billion. An additional couple of hundred million dollars in loans for specific projects have been provided during these five years by the Arab Fund for Social and Economic Development, the Abu Dhabi Fund for Economic Development, the Kuwait Fund for Arab Economic Development, and the Saudi Fund for Development. World Bank and IDA project loans and IMF commitments have totaled about $1 billion, while in July 1978, the IMF made a new three-year arrangement for drawings of 600 million. Loan commitments from Iran, Japan, and Europe have totaled about $1.8 billion. The United States resumed its aid program in 1974, and, following the September 1975 Sinai accord, the levels of assistance increased sharply. American assistance is extended within the overriding U.S. foreign policy objectives in the Middle East of a comprehensive peace and access to oil supplies. The United States believes that, given its strategic location and size and its influential relations with other Arab countries, current Egyptian government policies are effective means to reach these objectives. U.S. economic assistance amounted to $250 million during 1975, and has since run at an annual rate of about $950 million. About half of the U.S. assistance has gone to finance the imports of food and industrial equipment, raw materials and spare parts, and the other half has paid for specific agricultural, industrial, infrastructural, and social projects.[17]

STEADY INDUSTRIAL EXPANSION

In contrast to the dramatic growth within a few nonindustrial sectors, the recent progress in industry has been pedestrian. Industrial output, however, may have recovered from the depression it experienced during the early 1970s. While industrial output, reflected in constant prices, had grown by a fairly steady 7 percent per year in the period 1952–66, the growth rate fell to less than 5 percent during 1966–71 and below 4 percent in the years 1972 through 1974. During 1975, the industrial growth rate spurted close to 10 percent with the real increase in the output of private industrial firms exceeding 15 percent. For 1976 and 1977, the annual rates of growth in current prices were only about 12 percent, yielding real rates of increase of only about 5 percent. Private-sector firms fared a little better with nominal rates of growth of 27 and 5 percent respectively, yielding an average rate of real increase of about 8 percent for the two years.[18]

Industrial sectors experiencing particularly rapid growth in recent years are those involving metallurgical and leather products, as is shown in Table 5.2. The increases in other areas are steady and not at all impressive.

Export trends are presented in Table 5.3. Fairly significant increases have taken place in paper and paper products, and, to a lesser extent, in transport equipment, beverages, and footwear. Exports of chemicals (not shown) also

TABLE 5.2: Gross Value of Industrial Production* by Sector, 1970–76 (in £E million)

Products	1970/71	1972	1973	1974	1975	1976
Food	479.0	518.5	561.0	608.6	698.0	774.0
Public	376.0	410.0	445.5	481.6	548.4	591.7
Private	103.0	108.5	115.5	127.0	149.6	183.1
Textiles	490.9	525.4	546.9	603.3	690.2	755.8
Public	367.0	395.9	411.1	458.3	503.9	563.1
Private	123.9	129.5	135.8	145.0	186.3	192.7
Chemicals	127.6	135.1	139.7	195.5	267.4	252.5
Public	96.3	102.3	101.4	153.4	207.1	180.4
Private	31.3	32.8	38.0	42.1	60.3	72.5
Engineering and metals	200.0	250.3	244.1	319.6	385.5	446.2
Public	169.1	217.1	204.1	271.0	327.9	381.2
Private	30.9	33.2	40.1	48.6	57.6	65.0
Mining	6.0	7.1	7.2	5.7	7.0	7.7
Public	6.0	7.1	7.2	5.7	7.0	7.7
Woodworking products	33.6	36.0	38.6	39.3	39.8	60.4
Leather Products	25.4	39.0	56.8	60.2	86.6	162.2
Total	1,417.4	1,569.9	1,594.3	1,832.2	2,174.5	2,459.5
Public	1,060.0	1,181.7	1,169.3	1,370.0	1,594.3	1,742.1
Private	357.4	388.2	425.0	462.2	580.2	735.5

*Includes only industrial subsectors under Ministry of Industry, Petroleum and Mining, accounting for over 85 percent of the gross value of industrial production. Excluded are building materials, pulp and paper, and military factories.

Sources: The 1970/71 and 1972 rows from Business International, *Egypt, Business Gateway to the Middle East* (New York: Business International, 1976), p. 34; and remainder from Arthur D. Little, Inc., *An Assessment of Egypt's Industrial Sector*, Report to the Special Interagency Task Force Reviewing the U.S. Security Supporting Assistance Program for Egypt (Cambridge, MA; January 1978), p. 23.

TABLE 5.3: Principal Exports, 1970–76 (in £E million)

Products	1970	1971	1972	1973	1974	1975	1976
Raw cotton	147.9	175.0	162.0	161.9	279.1	201.0	154.8
Cotton yarn	35.6	35.6	42.6	44.2	65.1	63.0	57.6
Cotton fabrics	18.1	17.5	17.5	16.7	20.1	16.2	17.4
Cotton waste and others*	12.9	15.2	19.1	22.2	30.7	41.8	36.7
Sugar and sugar confectionery	4.4	7.4	2.5	5.2	11.5	15.4	11.4
Beverages and spirits	2.6	3.7	4.3	5.2	5.4	9.7	6.0
Paper and paper products	2.0	1.5	2.8	1.6	3.6	3.8	4.5
Raw hides, skins, footwear	5.9	5.8	7.2	7.9	11.0	19.3	9.7
Crude oil	15.3	1.9	20.3	36.9	23.9	23.1	109.8
Gasoline, kerosene, and fuel oil	0.5	0.3	1.8	1.5	0.2	5.7	10.9
Phosphate and manganese	1.4	1.2	1.0	0.6	1.8	2.2	2.2
Cement	1.7	5.9	3.7	4.6	2.4	1.2	0.6
Machinery and electric apparatus	1.5	2.4	3.3	1.7	1.7	2.2	1.1
Transport equipment	1.1	0.3	2.4	1.0	1.1	3.4	3.2
Iron, steel, and products thereof	3.5	3.7	5.6	4.1	7.8	10.3	4.8
Total	331	343	359	444	593	549	595

*Includes other fibers, raw and manufactured.
Source: National Bank of Egypt, *Economic Bulletin* (No. 3, 1977), Tables 2 b, c, d.

expanded markedly, particularly through private sector firms.[19] On the other hand, the export performance in machinery and electrical apparatuses and in transport equipment was disappointing. Exports of cement kept on falling until their disappearance in 1977, due to steadily declining production and the vigorous construction program. Rising domestic consumption also underlay the disappointing export performance for other commodities; other relevant factors are inadequate marketing efforts, poor quality, and noncompetitive prices due to increases in wages and other costs outstripping productivity improvements.[20]

Statistics on the production of individual industrial commodities are presented in Table 5.4. Marked increases in output have taken place in preserved fruits and vegetables, soft drinks, cars, refrigerators, TV sets, washing machines, motorcycles, gloves, caustic soda, nitrate fertilizer, and, to a less extent, salt, iron ore, iron products, and bicycles. A significant feature of industrial expansion, since 1973, is the apparently greater concentration on consumer goods. The major production increases recorded since 1973 have been in the "big-ticket" consumer items; the increases in output registered for equipment for agricultural, industrial, and construction use are less pronounced.

Table 2.10 and 2.11 of Chapter 2 shed some light on the industrial diversification which was achieved during the 1950s and 1960s. These tables demonstrate that higher than average growth had taken place in paper, rubber, chemicals, nonmetallic products, basic metals, simple machinery, and electrical appliances. Tables 5.5 and 5.6 are presented to demonstrate that chemicals, basic metals, machinery, and paper continue to be the high-growth sectors. Beverages, clothing, and transport equipment have also shown high growth rates. During the 1973–75 period, the significant increases took place in chemicals, coal products, basic metals, metallic products, machinery, transport equipment, beverages, and paper.

Table 5.7 is presented to give some idea of the comparative importance of the different industries over the last thirty years. The comparisons have to be considered rough since the data bases and compilation methods are not the same for the four sample years.

The period since 1973 is really too short for one to reach a definitive conclusion on industrial diversification. The output increases so far registered in the more sophisticated industrial products do not appear impressive, however, and there is an absence of reports in any of the special studies or periodicals on the introduction of new products. The progress in industry since 1973 can be labeled as steady, but not inspiring.

In searching for factors to explain the not very inspiring performance in most industrial sectors, Arthur D. Little, Inc. emphasizes the underutilized capacity created principally by poor maintenance and use of equipment, low labor productivity abetted by both overstaffing and poor supervision, and

TABLE 5.4: Output of Selected Industrial Products (in thousands of metric tons unless otherwise stated)

Products	Previous Peak Output and Year	1973	1974	1975	1976	1977	1978*
Spinning and weaving products							
Cotton yarn	179 (1972)	182	179	181	193	210	220
Cotton textiles	115 (1972)	118	120	122	138	905	940
Woolen yarn and fabrics	19 (1965)	11	11	12	13	—	—
Foodstuffs, etc.							
Sugar	610 (1972)	633	577	526	576	614	700
Cheese	135 (1972)	135	135	153	147	149	160
Preserved fruits and vegetables	26 (1971/72)	24	18	24	48	41	55
Cottonseed oil	158 (1971/72)	160	170	161	160	166	170
Oilseed cakes	733 (1965/66)	600	540	720	417	430	465
Soft drinks (millions of bottles)	751 (1964/65)	600	660	784	960	984	1,300
Beer (millions of liters)	30 (1972)	32	29	29	30	39	43
Cigarettes (billions)	23 (1972)	23	23	21	28	25	27
Dairy products	168 (1972)	174	177	194	176	—	—
Chemicals, etc.							
Soap	154 (1968)	143	183	219	227	—	—
Sulfuric acid	227 (1967/68)	23	30	36	28	27	36
Superphosphate	522 (1971/72)	419	465	520	493	513	530
Ammonium nitrate (31 percent nitrogen)	438 (1967/68)	210	320	400	530	1,258	695
Tires (thousands)	927 (1972)	860	814	923	859	903	795
Paper and cardboard	152 (1972)	149	131	146	92	—	—
Caustic soda	20 (1969)	14	14	37	37	—	—

TABLE 5.4: (Continued)

Engineering products							
Cars (units)	6,130 (1972)	5,590	8,169	11,576	9,799	12,817	12,880
Trucks and tractors (units)	2,956 (1972)	2,761	2,342	2,825	3,807	4,445	3,030
Buses (units)	1,155 (1965/66)	413	360	305	307	475	470
Refrigerators (thousands)	68 (1969/70)	39	55	109	112	129	130
Television sets (thousands)	84 (1966/67)	49	68	77	88	138	135
Metallurgical products							
Reinforcing bars	251 (1969/70)	226	232	219	202	230	275
Steel sections	135 (1968/69)	87	81	106	151	128	145
Steel sheets	179 (1972)	167	125	211	156	235	225
Cast iron products	54 (1962/63)	53	55	66	63	78	72
Cement	3,921 (1971)	3,617	3,263	3,579	3,362	—	—
Glass	21 (1971)	24	16	20	22	—	—
Mining products							
Phosphate	748 (1967/68)	540	499	428	392	468	445
Iron ore	553 (1965/66)	—	1,033	2,424	—	—	—
Salt	498 (1952)	656	1,302	1,087	1,242	—	—
Refined petroleum products	6,264 (1972)	6,623	6,882	8,614	9,950	10,302	—

*Estimated from figures for the first nine months of 1978.
Source: Ministry of Industry and Mining, Cairo, Egypt; and National Bank of Egypt, *Economic Bulletin* (No. 1, 1978), Table 5/4.

TABLE 5.5: Gross Value Added in Manufacturing, Mining, and Petroleum by Branch of Activity, 1969/70–1975 (£E million) (at constant 1969/70 factor cost)

Industry	1969/70	1970/1	1971/2	1973	1974	1975
Mining and quarrying (excl. petroleum)	7.8	7.5	7.8	8.3	8.8	10.3
Manufacturing:	506.7	552.0	574.8	574.2	601.4	657.7
Food industries	104.5	110.6	113.8	111.3	110.7	113.6
Beverages	4.9	5.3	6.3	6.2	6.8	8.9
Tobacco	14.2	15.5	17.6	20.0	20.5	23.0
Ginning and pressing	6.2	6.5	7.8	8.2	7.6	7.6
Spinning and weaving	114.7	126.4	128.0	118.6	120.3	130.6
Clothing and wearing apparel	22.9	28.2	28.6	40.3	41.7	36.3
Wood	15.8	17.1	17.0	16.3	16.6	16.7
Paper	9.8	11.5	12.4	12.7	13.2	16.5
Printing and publishing	14.5	15.0	15.5	15.6	15.7	16.4

TABLE 5.5: (Continued)

Leather	4.9	5.4	5.7	6.9	7.1	6.4
Rubber	5.4	6.3	5.8	5.5	5.4	6.8
Chemicals	54.9	59.7	64.1	55.8	64.0	78.5
Coal products	1.4	1.8	1.9	1.8	3.6	4.3
Nonmetallic	23.5	25.8	29.2	28.0	26.8	29.8
Basic metals	23.9	24.0	25.8	27.4	28.5	33.4
Metallic products	16.6	17.0	18.3	18.0	19.0	23.7
Nonelectrical machinery	6.4	8.8	8.1	7.5	7.5	9.0
Electrical machinery	16.9	17.7	17.8	18.3	20.6	25.9
Transport equipment	14.9	18.6	19.3	21.4	21.7	26.0
Miscellaneous	30.4	30.8	31.8	34.4	44.1	45.3
Petroleum sector:	63.7	75.3	67.6	64.9	61.6	83.8
Crude petroleum	53.9	60.4	45.8	32.0	28.3	45.8
Petroleum products	9.8	14.9	21.8	32.9	33.3	38.0

Source: Estimates obtained from Ministry of Planning, Cairo, Egypt

TABLE 5.6: Gross Value Added in Manufacturing, 1969/70–1975

Type of Industry	Percentages		
	1969/70	*1973*	*1975*
Food, beverages, tobacco	23.9	22.6	20.9
Textiles	27.8	27.5	25.1
Wood, paper, printing, leather, rubber, nonmetallic products	14.3	14.0	13.3
Chemicals, coal, petroleum products	12.8	14.9	17.4
Basic metals and metallic products	7.8	7.5	8.2
Machinery and transport equipment	7.4	7.8	8.7
Miscellaneous	6.0	5.7	6.4
Total	100.0	100.0	100.0

Type of Industry	Percentage Rates of Growth	
	Total Increase 1969/70–75	*Average Annual Rate of Increase 1969/70–75*
Food, beverages, tobacco	17.7	3.01
Textiles	21.3	3.58
Wood, paper, printing, leather, rubber, nonmetallic products	25.3	4.18
Chemicals, coal, petroleum	82.7	11.58
Basic metals and products	41.0	6.44
Machinery and transport equipment	59.4	8.85
Crude petroleum	31.5	5.11
Mining and quarrying	32.0	5.18
Miscellaneous industries	49.0	7.52
Total manufacturing	34.7	5.56
Total industry incl. mining & petroleum	30.0	4.89

Source: Derived from Table 5.5

various types of supply bottlenecks.[21] These bottlenecks and factors are aggravated by poor plant and inventory management, shortage of storage capacity, and inefficient government decision-making in the allocation of funds for spare parts and materials. There is also a propensity to install excessively modern and sophisticated equipment even for simple operations, with a resulting low degree of productivity.

One of the most serious drawbacks cited above—low utilization of industrial capacity, due to shortages of raw materials, spare parts, and equipment—has been tackled forcefully by United States economic assistance. American assistance to finance the imports of this material and equipment has totaled $1.2 billion through the middle of 1978 and has gone a long way to alleviate such shortages as tallow for the soap industry, tin plate for the canning industry, and coking coal for the steel industry. As a result of such assistance, the average rate of capacity utilization throughout Egyptian industry has risen from 65 percent in 1974 to 85 percent in 1976.[22] In a way, it is surprising that such effective assistance combined with the much more favorable environment for business generally has not resulted in a faster rate of growth in industrial production.

It is probably true that too little time has elapsed since 1973 to promote a really vigorous industrial expansion, and the underpinnings may have already been laid for a breakthrough soon. Egypt's 1978–82 Five Year Plan anticipates that the average annual rate of industrial growth may reach 13 percent. Since this rate is so much higher than ever before experienced in Egypt, its realization will be difficult, probably quite impossible, during this time period. A detailed analysis of this projection will be offered in Chapter 7, but meantime a brief listing of some of the favorable recent economic developments which promise a faster rate of industrial growth will be given here. The building of essential infrastructure facilities in such areas as power and telecommunications has been stepped up. A major example in power is the USAID-financed $275 million project to build three power stations at Ismailia, Talkha, and Helwan with a combined generating capacity of 600,-000 kilowatts. An example in telecommunications is the IDA-supported $210 million project to install 226,000 local exchange lines and 5,000 trunk exchange lines for long distance telephone services, and a new 3,000-line exchange in Cairo to expand telex services. Several pipelines are being built to fuel industrial development; an example is the natural gas line being built to carry one million cubic meters of gas per day from the Abu Gharadig field to fertilizer plants in Suez.[23]

Examples of recent industrial developments involving foreign investors, such as new aluminum and tractor plants, were cited in the last chapter. A major effort is being made by the Egyptian government to expand cement production capacity. USAID financing is assisting in the building of one cement plant with an annual capacity of one million tons. With the completion

TABLE 5.7: Gross Value Added in Manufacturing Industries, Selected Years, Current Prices

Industry	1947		1966/67		1969/70		1975	
	£E Million	Percent	£E Million	Percent	£E Million	Percent	£E Million	Percent
Food	10.5	20.7	44.0	12.1	104.5	20.4	140.0	17.5
Beverages	1.7	3.4	3.9	1.1	4.9	0.9	12.0	1.5
Tobacco	5.4	10.6	13.8	3.8	14.2	2.7	27.6	3.4
Textiles	21.8	43.0	120.6	33.2	120.9	23.6	168.0	21.0
Wearing apparel	1.1	2.1	17.4	4.8	22.9	4.4	50.7	6.3
Wood	0.1	0.2	3.8	1.1	15.8	3.0	18.7	
Furniture	0.8	1.8	9.2	2.5				
Paper	0.5	0.9	9.1	2.5	9.8	1.9	22.0	2.0
Printing	1.1	2.2	7.1	2.0	14.5	2.8	18.5	2.0
Leather	0.5	1.0	2.5	0.7	4.9	0.9	9.8	1.0
Rubber	0.2	0.4	3.0	0.8	5.4	1.0	9.2	1.0
Chemicals	2.1	4.2	39.4	10.8	54.9	10.6	96.3	12.0
Petroleum	1.0	2.0	16.0	4.4	11.2	2.2	−23.9	−3.0

TABLE 5.7: (Continued)

Nonmetallic	1.4	2.8	15.6	4.3	23.5	4.5	40.1	5.0
Basic metals	0.2	0.3	12.4	3.4	23.9	4.6	52.2	6.9
Metallic products	1.7	3.4	15.5	4.3	16.6	3.2	28.0	3.0
Nonelectric machinery	—	0.0	3.9	1.1	6.4	1.2	10.0	1.0
Electric machinery	—	—	10.8	3.0	16.9	3.3	33.2	4.0
Transport equipment	0.3	0.3	9.8	2.7	14.9	2.9	32.3	4.0
Miscellaneous	0.3	0.5	5.1	1.4	30.4	5.9	56.0	7.0
	50.7	100.0	362.9	100.0	516.5	100.0	800.7	100.0

Composition of Gross Value Added in Percentages by Categories of Industries, 1947, 1966/67, 1969/70, and 1975

	1947	1966/67	1969/70	1975
Category A (Basic consumer goods)	79.8	55.0	51.6	49.7
Category B (Intermediate industries)	19.7	38.2	40.6	40.6
Category C (Consumer durables/equipment)	0.5	6.8	7.4	9.3

Source: 1947 and 1966/67, Robert Mabro and Samir Radwan, *The Industrialization of Egypt 1939–1973–Policy and Performance* (New York: Oxford University Press, 1976), p. 101; 1969/70 and 1975, Ministry of Planning, Cairo, Egypt.

of three more plants in the planning stages and the expansion of others, the annual production of cement should rise from less than 4 million tons in 1977 to 8.4 million tons in the 1980s. A $60 million USAID contract is financing the import of furnaces and equipment for glass factories to permit the annual production of flat glass to expand seven-fold to 100,000 tons, when the factories become fully operational by the mid-1980s. USAID is also financing a pulp and paper production facility and is extending major loans through the Development Industrial Bank for relending to private and public enterprises to help finance their expansion plans.[24] The Egyptian government is taking steps to establish new units or to expand facilities in the fields of fertilizers, chemicals, metallurgy, and mining. With all of these efforts by the Egyptian government and foreign donors, and, with the gradual removal of the growth constraints as described in the next chapter, much greater participation by foreign and Egyptian business enterprise in Egypt's development plans is in prospect. The result could well be an acceleration of Egypt's industrial growth by the mid-1980s. This acceleration combined with the predicted spectacular growth in shipping, tourism, emigrant remittances, and petroleum activity could then in turn create a mutually reinforcing pattern of further business interest and participation and continued rapid economic growth.

NOTES

1. See, for example, Robert Mabro and Samir Radwan, *The Industrialization of Egypt 1939–1973—Policy and Performance* (New York: Oxford University Press, 1976), p. 39.

2. Recent research has lowered the estimates for the Egyptian population during the nineteenth century, as explained in Justin A. McCarthy, "The Nineteenth Century Egyptian Population," *Middle Eastern Studies*, Vol. 12 (October 1976), pp. 1–39.

3. See Donald C. Mead, *Growth and Structural Change in the Egyptian Economy* (Homewood, Illinois: Richard D. Irwin, 1967), p. 21.

4. A good description of the minimal prospects for further progress in Egyptian agriculture appears in Charles Issawi, "Egypt since 1800: A Study in Lopsided Development," *Journal of Economic History* (March 1961), pp. 14–16.

5. See Mead, op. cit., p. 75.

6. See Mabro and Radwan, op. cit., p. 104, and "Ominous Signs on the Farm," *Financial Times* (July 31, 1978).

7. FMC Corporation was earlier involved with installing special irrigation pipes in newly reclaimed land, while a recently announced joint venture in agriculture is Coca-Cola's agreement in 1977 to cooperate with an Egyptian company to grow oranges near Ismailia.

8. As reported in "Suez Canal for All Ages," *Financial Times* (July 31, 1978).

9. See, for example, *Petroleum Economist* (July 1977) and "Shipping Returns to Suez," *Financial Times* (July 31, 1978).

10. This agreement between the Suez Canal Authority and container owners was cited in *Financial Times* (June 29, 1977).

11. I used, as main sources, the tables in National Bank of Egypt, *Economic Bulletin* (No. 3, 1976), p. 265, and (No. 3, 1977), pp. 252, 253. I adjusted the calculations to take account

of the fact that the overall growth rates for 1975 and 1976 have recently been revised downward from the 10.9 and 9.8 rates shown to 9.8 and 7.4 percent respectively. Since the 1976 downward revision is especially sharp, the result of my calculations for that year should be considered as a rough approximation only.

12. Details of the Suez Canal expansion plans appeared in the *Journal of Commerce* (August 26, 1977) and the World Bank press release of August 11, 1977.

13. See National Bank of Egypt, *Economic Bulletin* (No. 3, 1976), p. 261, and "Vast Tourism Potential," *Financial Times* (July 31, 1978).

14. World Bank, *Economic Report on Egypt* (Washington, D.C.: April 1978).

15. This account of Egypt's petroleum experience is largely based on "Steady Income from Oil," *Financial Times* (July 31, 1978).

16. These production estimates are from ibid., and National Bank of Egypt, *Economic Bulletin* (No. 2, 1977), pp. 134–35.

17. Information on the objectives and goals of U.S. economic assistance in Egypt is given in Agency for International Development, *U.S. Economic Assistance to Egypt—A Report of A Special Interagency Task Force* (Washington, D.C.: February 1978).

18. Arthur D. Little, Inc. in *An Assessment of Egypt's Industrial Sector,* Report to the Special Interagency Task Force Reviewing the U.S. Security Supporting Assistance Program for Egypt (Cambridge, MA, January, 1978), pp. 22, arrives at the conclusion that the growth in industrial output was an estimated 10 percent in 1975 and 1976. This assessment is corroborated for 1975 in the tabular information supplied on page 23 and in National Bank of Egypt, "Follow-up of Egypt's Economic and Social Development During 1975," *Economic Bulletin* (No. 3, 1976), p. 265. On the other hand, the assessment for 1976 is contradicted in the same page 23 table and in the Bank's "Follow-up of the 1976 State Plan," *Economic Bulletin* (No. 3, 1977), p. 252. The bank lists the 1976 increase in industrial and mining output at 1975 prices as 5 percent. "The National Economy—1977," National Bank of Egypt, *Economic Bulletin* (No. 1, 1978), p. 16, indicates that the 1977 increase in industrial output was similar to the 1976 rate of increase.

Little's assessment on their page 72, that the output of the private manufacturing sector increased by an annual average of 15 percent in real terms during 1975 and 1976, is confirmed in Table 5.2.

19. Delwin A. Roy, *Private Industry Sector Development in Egypt: An Analysis of Trends, 1973–1977,* Report to the Special Interagency Task Force Reviewing the U.S. Security Supporting Assistance Program for Egypt (Washington, D.C.: AID, January, 1978), pp. 8–9, shows that the export performance of private industrial firms has been infinitely better than that of public firms. For example, during 1975, the industrial exports of private firms rose by over 8 percent, while the exports of public sector firms declined by 8 percent.

20. These factors are discussed in Egypt-U.S. Business Council, *Report on Foreign Investment in Egypt* (Washington, D.C.: 1976), Appendix 1, pp. iv–v.

21. These factors are discussed in sector detail in Little, op. cit., pp. 25–28 and 98–100.

22. See Agency for International Development, op. cit., pp. 7, 52.

23. These are examples of recent infrastructure projects reported in the regional periodicals and summarized in the National Foreign Trade Council's *Middle East and North African Notes.*

24. These examples of recent industrial developments appear in ibid., and in Agency for International Development, op. cit., pp. 20, 27.

REMOVAL OF
ENVIRONMENTAL
CONSTRAINTS

The conclusion reached in Chapter 3 was that a vastly improved legal framework for foreign investment activity had evolved in Egypt during the 1970s. While some foreign investors might desire further improvements and clarifications, the present legal framework is on the whole quite favorable and no longer poses a serious obstacle to the entry of new foreign capital.

On the other hand, environmental factors have been more serious impediments, at least until recently. These impediments have been the unsettled regional political situation, the uncertain and occasionally drawn-out relationships with the government, inadequate infrastructural facilities, shortages in capital and foreign exchange, and some tightness in certain skills. Progress is being made in resolving all these difficulties, and there are good prospects that programs now underway will soon substantially remove these environmental factors as constraints on significant economic growth and foreign investor interest.

REGIONAL CONSIDERATIONS

The October War of 1973 brought about a transformation in the very attitude of the Egyptian policy-makers. The rather favorable political and military outcome of that war permitted the Egyptians to shake their previous inferiority complex and to deal realistically with the Israelis. Two disengagement agreements followed in 1974 and 1975, and President Sadat launched a bold peace initiative in November 1977 with a precedent-shattering personal visit to Jerusalem. Serious negotiations took place over the ensuing ten months, punctuated by occasional angry outbursts and the frequent assumption of extreme public positions for bargaining purposes. The culmination was the Camp David accords signed by Presidents Carter and Sadat and Prime Minister Begin on September 17, 1978, to be followed by a peace treaty between Egypt and Israel.

The negotiations between Egypt and Israel marked a significant improvement in the regional political situation and could well be the initial stepping stone to a durable peace in the area. A package deal to peace among all the parties to the thirty-year-old Arab-Israeli conflict was not a practicable early possibility. When the Egyptians, Americans, and Israelis reached agreement at Camp David they not only kept their own interests in mind but also established a model for later accords to involve the other parties in the area.

The removal of tensions on the Sinai front by itself alleviated much of the fear felt by potential foreign investors in Egypt. A large-scale war in the area does not appear to be a military possibility without the participation of Egypt. On the other hand, a durable peace is not possible, and political instability and small-scale military outbursts will result, if the tensions of Syrians, Jordanians, Palestinians, and perhaps also Lebanese are not assuaged. Foreign investments largely dependent upon export prospects need an environment of relative regional stability. If much more complete common market arrangements were to emerge, so much the better.

The political aspect of Egypt's investment climate earlier received much emphasis, with many foreign investors stressing the uncertain regional political situation as being among the most important reasons for their hesitancy.[1] Now that substantial progress has been made on the political front, it would be interesting to evaluate the importance of this factor, among others. Lucien Bruggeman, the Allis-Chalmers official who served as "investment development officer" for nine months at the Egyptian Economic Mission, is emphatic on the overwhelming importance of political stability. Several weeks before the Camp David accords, Bruggeman stated: "Without a peace settlement in the Middle East, or at least significant movement in that direction, not many American corporations are going to be seriously interested in investing in Egypt. . . . If there are indications of a settlement, however, 'the higher interest' of corporate executives will come into play and investment opportunities will be closely pursued, irrespective of the other obstacles which may still exist."

A different opinion was voiced during a seminar on Egypt sponsored by the National Foreign Trade Council on September 29, 1978. In a luncheon conversation, Dr. Ibrahim Oweiss, Director of the Egyptian Economic Mission, asked the eight representatives of multinational firms present at the table whether foreign investors will be much more disposed to invest in Egypt now that the political uncertainties had largely been settled with the Camp David accords. The business representatives each stated that he thought not; while the political factor is important, foreign investors might not move forward eagerly until the other serious environmental obstacles are taken care of.[2]

I concur in the latter view. The resolution of the regional political difficulties is a necessary but not sufficient condition for attracting much more foreign investment to Egypt. The Egyptian authorities are certainly to be commended for the significant progress made in a political direction; additional progress is also needed in tackling such other environmental aspects as relationships with the government, infrastructure, capital, and skills.

RELATIONSHIPS WITH THE GOVERNMENT

Foreign investors experience two main difficulties in securing agreement from the Egyptian government for launching their projects. The first difficulty is the length of time required for the many necessary contacts, and the second is the discrepancy between various basic governmental attitudes toward foreign investors.

The approval process is lengthy because of the multiplicity of agencies involved. One appraisal in 1975 counted one-hundred eighty different steps required between the application for project approval and incorporation of the company. This situation is compounded by the lack of fixed criteria for use by government officials in reaching decisions or determining the extent of various incentives. Many foreign investors get the impression that some of the reviews to which their proposals are subjected are directionless and without any apparent meaning.[3]

The lack of specific criteria for decision-making and the many officials involved often lead to diverse and even conflicting interpretations. For example, one investor has reported receiving tax holiday proposals from different officials ranging from 3 to 8 years. Another reported being informed first that a lease for a land site would be required to obtain free zone status, only to be told by another official that approval for free zone status must precede the granting of a lease. A third investor believes that getting approvals on remittances and on payments of technical service fees and royalties is frequently difficult and depends on the whim of the responsible official in charge at any given moment. This lack of coordination between officials of different agencies and even within the same agency is worsened by the frequent ignorance of the proper delegation of responsibility within the Egyptian government for implementing various aspects of the investment laws. The government hiring and firing practices based on policies to provide employment outlets for all graduates each year and to assure lifetime tenure have resulted in overstaffed offices. This overstaffing and the uncertain delimitation of responsibilities have often caused an endless shuffling of papers and the involvement of extra officials to reach a decision on each separate clearance. Thus the problem is not merely the long delays sometimes experienced in the decision-making process, but the fact that foreign investors are often unable to plan ahead with any confidence on the steps which might need to be taken with respect to any proposed investment.[4] This very uncertainty causes some foreign investors to shy away from making the initial application.

The other major bureaucratic problem has been the conflict in policy orientation between the Egyptian leadership and the lower levels of the government. Senior officials are clearly committed to the opening up of the economy to private enterprise, both local and foreign. The bulk of the bureaucracy, however, has been trained since the late 1950s to stifle private initiative and to control all aspects of the economy, and these habits of state paternalism cannot be changed overnight. The widespread uncertainty as to how to apply Law No. 43 to potential investors has created a tendency among working-level Egyptian officials to follow precedents from the preliberalization era. Consequently, the Western-oriented intentions of the top government bureaucrats to be responsive to the needs of foreign investors have often been sabotaged by uncooperative attitudes and cumbersome procedures at lower echelons.

The bureaucracy problem in Egypt, while serious, may not be any worse than in the average developing country. Some steady progress has been made since about 1975 in loosening up bureaucratic controls. The number of steps in the approval process has been cut drastically, and the umbrella organization—the General Authority for Foreign Investment—has undergone reorganization. The Authority has acted more quickly in its handling of pending cases, and the clearance process with other agencies has also apparently been expedited. There is not yet a "one-stop" service for considering foreign investments, but at least by 1977, separate offices for labor, taxation, law, and passports had been added to the headquarters building of the Authority to help serve the needs of new investors. Considerable efforts have been made to educate the staff of the Authority and other government agencies in modern methods of project appraisal, and there is an expectation that, in time, the paternalistic attitudes rampant in the bureaucracy will be modified.[5]

As described in Chapter 3, a major step in loosening up bureaucratic controls was the passage of Law No. 111 of September 18, 1975. This law abolished the General Organizations for industrial subsectors. The successor Supreme Sector Councils do not interfere in ordinary managerial decision-making as had often been the case with the General Organizations, but rather review the broad outlines of the companies' budgets, investment programs, and proposed output levels for the major commodities. New investment projects requiring funds of less than £E500,000 may go ahead without government approval if the necessary capital is available within the firm, and new products can be introduced if there is no interference with the planned output targets for the original products and if the required funds and materials can easily be obtained. Cumbersome procedures and long delays are still sometimes experienced by plant managers in dealings with the relevant ministries regarding major expansion plans.[6]

Some government controls are still rather onerous. While the monopoly of state-owned companies in foreign trade has been broken, a continuing bureaucratic restriction concerns price controls over a number of strategic commodities, such as cloth, bread, sugar, edible oil, soap, and utilities. There is also extensive governmental supervision of employment policies, pressure sometimes being exerted to take on excess employees. There is also a general prohibition against laying off redundant or inefficient employees. The government has, however, announced its intention to reduce the number of items under price control from the present 80 or so to 15–20, and the liberalization of government controls in other areas is planned. For example, action has been taken or plans have been announced to invite individuals and private firms to invest in some state-sector companies, such as the Nasr Automobile Company and a major cement plant.[7]

Two recent indicators attest to a relative contraction of the public sector. In 1974, the private sector accounted for only 10 percent of the gross domestic product, while in 1978, it accounted for 17 percent, and Egyptian officials estimate that this percentage share will expand to 25 percent by the 1980s. Whereas all university graduates were once guaranteed government jobs immediately upon graduation, many of them now wait for eighteen months or more to fill the annual vacancies now cut down to 15,000. The long waiting period is occasioned by the fact that the number of applicants is now six times as high as in the past.[8]

INFRASTRUCTURAL FACILITIES

There have been many complaints by foreign investors about the deficiencies in Egypt's infrastructural facilities. Despite a post-1973 expansion in investment, serious dissatisfaction exists with the services rendered in the area of telecommunications and, to a lesser extent, port facilities, railways, and power distribution. The infrastructural deficiencies appear to be caused by insufficient investments as well as low user fees combined with excess staffing.

Telephone service has become increasingly inadequate, both in quantity and quality. While the number of installed telephones has been increasing steadily to some 400,000 by 1978, the waiting list for new telephones has soared. In 1968, there were but 15,500 waiting applicants; by 1976, the number rose to 268,000, and many people have been told they may have to wait as much as fourteen years before they are likely to get a telephone. Business firms desiring a telephone must either rent premises with a telephone currently installed, press for special consideration, or resign themselves to a long wait. Much of the existing telephone equipment is so old that placing calls is a major headache, with many poor connections and wrong numbers.[9]

Progress in telecommunications has been impeded by inadequate investments. During 1973 and 1974, Egypt invested a minuscule 0.19 percent of GDP in telecommunications and even in 1975, the proportion rose to only 0.39 percent. By contrast, this proportion for most developing countries is more than 0.6 percent. The main reason for the inadequacy in investment is the low rate structure. Except for a small increase in the annual rentals for telexes in July 1976, telephone rates have not been increased since 1966.[10] Secondly, the government's employment policy has led to excess staffing, and the resulting higher costs have inhibited the accumulation of investment funds.

The Egyptian government is aware of the widespread dissatisfaction among local and foreign businessmen with the calamitous character of existing telephone services. Several American companies, including Continental Telephone International, have completed studies on both short and long-term remedies. In order to finance a three-year $210 million telecommunications project, the International Development Association is lending $53 million, the L. M. Ericsson Company $40.5 million, and the United States, France, and Saudi Arabia lesser amounts. The equipment for this and smaller projects includes coaxial cables, multiplex equipment, 5,000 trunk exchange lines, and microwave services are also being upgraded through the provision of 226,000 local exchange lines. For the longterm, American companies have suggested a five-year program, costing $3 billion, to revamp existing equipment and to increase telephone lines to one million; a further fifteen-year program, costing another $17 billion, would increase the number of lines to five million. Such a long-term telephone project would also have a significant impact on the development of industries and sophisticated skills. Whereas the country has been producing wires and cables for some time and recently went on to manufacture crossbar telephone switching equipment and telephone receivers under license from L. M. Ericsson, the long-term project will also involve elaborate training programs and the local manufacture of electronic exchanges and other sophisticated telephone equipment.[11] With the mammoth size of the overall project, the Egyptian government is taking its time in making final arrangements with international contractors, but the extent of its commitment can be judged by the impressive allocation of £E480 million to be invested in telecommunications under the 1978–82 Plan.

Compared with the telecommunications situation, the deficiencies in the other infrastructural areas are not nearly so serious. Egypt has a surplus of power-generating capacity with the completion of the Aswan High Dam, and there is a growing surplus of oil and gas. The power deficiencies rather relate to generation at major user sites and to transmission and distribution facilities.

American financial assistance has been devoted to upgrading regional and national grids and to increasing generating capacity by 600,000 kilowatts in the Suez region and in the industrial centers of Helwan and Talka. The raising of local investment funds is hampered, as in other infrastructural facilities, by a frozen rate structure—rates have not been increased since 1970, with the price of fuel burned in the production of electricity being calculated at pre-1973 prices rather than current international prices.

In the transport sector, shortages of rolling stock and port equipment prevent the efficient handling of the increasing cargo tonnages. Egypt is currently importing dozens of new locomotives,

A major rehabilitation of the port of Alexandria is being carried out with the assistance of the World Bank and Japan. Substantial improvements to the Suez Canal ports are also planned. In the road sector, a $70 million mile-long tunnel under the canal is to become operational by 1980. The £E1.6 billion allocated under the 1978–82 plan promises to alleviate the remaining deficiencies in the transport sector. These planned investments include £E310 million for railways, and £E140 million for ocean transport and ports.

CAPITAL AND FOREIGN EXCHANGE AVAILABILITIES

Shortages of capital and foreign exchange were a serious obstacle to industrial and economic development during the 1960s, as noted in Chapter 2. Generous foreign assistance is currently eliminating this development constraint, while rapidly rising income is expected before long from a number of special sources. This surge in income, combined with possible progress in raising the total of domestic savings, should provide adequate capital and foreign exchange to promote significant economic growth and stimulate a favorable investment climate.

Table 6.1 plainly shows the sharp rise in total investments since 1973. Gross fixed investments jumped from £E462 million in 1973 to £E1,691 million in 1977. During the same period, investment funds devoted to industry, petroleum, and mining soared to almost five times the former total. There has been a corresponding explosion in the import surplus, shown in the row of Table 6.2 labeled "Excess of imports over exports." As a percentage of the gross domestic product, this excess was under 2 percent during the 1950s, and then rose to approximately 4 or 5 percent during most of the 1960s and early 1970s. During the 1974–77 period, however, this rate soared to 13 percent. Obviously, there is at present no shortage of capital and foreign exchange.

However, this sharp rise in the balance of payments deficit and the related greater dependence on foreign sources for the financing of investments has its own dangers. The very high levels of current foreign assistance cannot be considered a long-term feature of the Egyptian economic scene. These levels are justified as a transitional measure to help pave the way for peace in the area and on the expectation that local funds will be generated over the next few years to take up some of the slack.

In analyzing the domestic mobilization of investment funds, the key ratios given in Table 6.2 are total investments and domestic savings as percentages of the GDP. Impressive progress with respect to the first ratio has recently been made with I/GDP jumping from roughly 13 or 14 percent during the 1950s, 1960s, and early 1970s to about 23 percent during the 1974–77 period. Nearly the entire increase, however, was due to the sharp rise in foreign assistance. Domestic savings as a percentage of the GDP actually showed a steadily falling trend through 1974, from mostly 14 or 15 percent during the period 1952–1967, to around 8 or 9 percent thereafter, to a low of 5.4 percent during 1974. There has been a recovery during the 1975–77 period to near historical levels. While the 1977 figure of 15 percent might be subject to later downward revision, the government hopes in its 1978–82 Plan that the domestic savings ratio will rise to at least 20 percent by 1982.

A number of chronic difficulties may impede the Egyptians from accomplishing this 20 percent savings objective.[12] The major reason in the past for a falling savings rate was the rapid rise in public consumption. As a percentage of the GDP, public consumption was under 20 percent prior to 1967, and then rose steadily to 28 percent by 1973. Public savings correspondingly went down from 12.5 percent of the GDP in 1970/71 to less than 1 percent in 1975, despite a commendable effort at increasing tax revenues. Rising military spending, overstaffing, and a continuing high rate of increase in population contributed to the growth in public spending, while controlled prices at artificially low levels and other bureaucratic inefficiencies have prevented the generation of significant corporate savings in both the public and private sectors. Low interest rates and high taxes on interest and dividends have stifled individual savings.

The share of public consumption in the GDP has recently gone down from the peak of 28 percent in 1973 to 21 percent in 1977. While the cost-of-living subsidies remain high, the recent improvements in peace prospects in the area and the liberalization policies have acted as a brake on public spending. Greater decentralization in decision-making has to some extent enabled private entrepreneurs to pursue higher profits and generate more investment funds. Private savings and investments have been further encouraged by the reopening of the stock exchanges in Cairo and Alexandria and by making the earnings from savings tax exempt. Interest rates were raised in May 1977 and again in June 1978 to reasonably attractive levels for savers.

Continuing progress in controlling rises in public consumption, in eliminating rigidities in prices, subsidies, and interest rates, and in stimulating

TABLE 6.1: Gross Fixed Investment by Sector—at Current Prices (in millions of Egyptian pounds)

	1955/56	*1960/61*
Agriculture	7.0	16.6
Irrigation and drainage	11.7	21.6
Industry, petroleum, and mining	49.8	67.8
Electricity	9.7	5.6
Construction	—	—
Transportation and communication	25.1	74.8
Trade and finance	—	—
Housing	54.6	19.1
Public utilities	5.1	7.7
Other services	13.9	19.8
Less: Expenditure for purchased land	−4.8	−7.4
Gross Fixed Investment	172.1	225.6
Public Sector	—	—
Private Sector	—	—

(As percentages of Gross Fixed Investment)

	1955/56	*1960/61*
Agriculture	4.1	7.4
Irrigation and drainage	6.8	9.6
Industry, petroleum, and mining	28.9	30.1
Electricity	5.6	2.5
Construction	—	—
Transportation and communication	14.6	33.1
Trade and finance	—	—
Housing	31.7	8.5
Public utilities	3.0	3.4
Other services	8.1	8.7
Expenditure for purchase of land	−2.8	−3.3
Gross Fixed Investment	100.0	100.0
Public Sector	—	—
Private Sector	—	—

Source: Estimates obtained from Ministry of Planning and Central Agency for Public Mobilization and Statistics, Cairo, Egypt.

1965/66	1966/67	1967/68	1968/69	1969/70	1970/71
30.7	31.3	24.9	25.6	27.0	27.9
51.6	50.9	31.6	42.0	34.3	25.4
100.6	98.4	80.8	101.1	123.1	125.7
61.1	69.3	62.9	31.9	27.3	23.1
6.8	3.9	2.0	2.6	3.4	8.9
53.1	46.1	38.3	69.5	71.4	81.2
2.7	2.6	0.7	2.7	3.6	9.5
47.5	42.3	41.7	46.9	36.5	26.5
12.4	8.6	4.2	5.8	10.9	16.8
17.3	12.4	10.9	15.4	18.0	16.0
−6.4	−7.0	−5.6	−10.3	−5.2	−6.0
377.3	358.8	292.3	333.2	350.8	355.5
349.6	329.4	266.0	290.9	312.9	314.5
27.7	29.4	26.3	42.3	37.9	41.0
8.2	8.6	8.5	7.6	7.7	7.9
13.6	14.2	10.8	12.6	9.8	7.1
26.7	27.4	27.6	30.3	35.1	35.4
16.2	19.3	21.5	9.6	7.8	6.5
1.8	1.1	0.7	0.7	1.0	2.5
14.1	12.9	13.1	20.5	20.4	22.9
0.7	0.7	0.2	1.0	1.0	2.7
12.6	11.8	14.3	14.1	10.4	7.5
3.3	2.4	1.4	1.6	3.1	4.7
4.6	3.5	3.7	4.5	5.1	4.5
−1.8	−1.9	−1.8	−2.5	−1.4	−1.7
100.0	100.0	100.0	100.0	100.0	100.0
92.6	91.8	91.0	87.3	89.3	88.5
7.4	8.2	9.0	12.7	10.7	11.5

TABLE 6.1: (Continued)

	1971/72	1972
Agriculture	22.3	28.3
Irrigation and drainage	21.6	22.0
Industry, petroleum, and mining	140.0	119.7
Electricity	21.3	26.3
Construction	5.5	3.9
Transportation and communication	79.6	100.1
Trade and finance	11.0	3.0
Housing	29.8	40.0
Public utilities	16.9	13.0
Other services	21.5	26.0
Less: Expenditure for purchased land	−4.5	−4.0
Gross Fixed Investment	365.0	378.3
Public Sector	325.0	337.3
Private Sector	40.0	41.0

(As percentages of Gross Fixed Investment)

	1971/72	1972
Agriculture	6.1	7.5
Irrigation and drainage	5.9	5.8
Industry, petroleum, and mining	38.4	31.6
Electricity	5.8	6.9
Construction	1.5	1.0
Transportation and communication	21.8	26.5
Trade and finance	3.0	0.8
Housing	8.1	10.6
Public utilities	4.7	3.4
Other services	5.9	6.9
Expenditure for purchase of land	−1.2	−1.1
Gross Fixed Investment	100.0	100.0
Public Sector	89.0	89.2
Private Sector	11.0	10.8

1973	1974	1975	1976	1977
35.2	32.7	42.4	99.4	132.0
22.4	21.5	41.7	—	
154.3	234.0	394.1	560.8	722.0
30.3	30.0	49.3	48.5	52.0
5.0	10.6	24.8	48.0	9.0
123.0	187.0	385.5	347.9	453.0
2.7	5.2	9.8	23.2	18.0
40.3	51.5	169.3	109.3	144.0
22.8	28.7	39.3	44.6	57.0
29.2	43.9	71.8	62.6	73.0
−3.2	−4.9	—	−19.3	−19.0
462.4	640.0	1,228.0	1,325.0	1,691.0
424.4	612.5	1,051.5	1,089.0	1,436.0
38.0	27.5	176.5	236.0	255.0
7.6	5.1	3.5	7.5	8.0
4.9	3.4	3.4	—	
33.4	36.6	32.1	42.3	43.0
6.6	4.7	4.0	3.7	3.0
1.1	1.7	2.0	3.6	1.0
26.6	29.2	31.4	26.3	27.0
0.6	0.8	0.8	1.7	1.0
8.7	8.0	13.8	8.3	9.0
4.9	4.5	3.2	3.4	3.0
6.3	6.8	5.8	4.7	4.0
−0.7	−0.8	—	−1.5	−1.0
100.0	100.0	100.0	100.0	100.0
91.9	95.7	85.6	82.2	85.0
8.1	4.3	14.4	17.8	15.0

TABLE 6.2: Share of Consumption and Savings in GDP (in millions of Egyptian pounds)

	1947	1952/53	1955/56
Total Resources		883.7	1,066.6
GDP at current factor cost		806.0	965.0
Net indirect taxes		62.4	88.9
GDP at market prices		868.4	1,053.9
Exports		234.0	258.2
Imports		249.3	270.9
Total Consumption		765.1	894.5
Public consumption		142.8	182.0
Private consumption		622.3	712.5
Gross Domestic Investment		118.6	172.1
Fixed investment		—	—
Change in stocks		—	—
Total Expenditures		883.7	1,066.6

Share of Main Aggregates in GDP (%)

	1947	1952/53	1955/56
Total Consumption	91.2	88.1	84.9
Public consumption	7.5	16.4	17.3
Private consumption	83.7	71.7	67.6
Total investment	12.0	13.6	16.3
Domestic savings	8.6	11.9	15.1
Exports	—	26.9	24.5
Imports	—	28.7	25.7
Excess of imports over exports	3.4	1.7	1.2

Source: Ministry of Planning, Cairo, Egypt, except for 1947 figures which are from Hansen and Nashashibi, *Foreign Trade Regimes and Economic Development: Egypt* (New York: National Bureau of Economic Research, Columbia University Press, 1975), p. 13.

1960/61	1965/66	1966/67	1967/68	1968/69	1969/70
1,477.9	2,572.1	2,581.4	2,669.9	2,767.0	3,151.6
1,363.5	2,138.2	2,194.9	2,202.7	2,339.4	2,663.0
95.8	321.3	350.1	356.5	342.2	375.7
1,459.3	2,459.5	2,545.0	2,559.2	2,681.6	3,038.7
280.4	375.7	378.8	258.1	322.6	434.4
299.0	488.3	415.2	368.8	408.0	547.3
1,252.3	2,126.0	2,195.8	2,327.6	2,448.8	2,705.8
255.9	486.9	499.8	584.1	619.3	713.9
996.4	1,639.1	1,696.0	1,743.5	1,829.5	1,991.9
225.6	446.1	385.6	342.3	318.2	445.8
—	377.3	358.8	292.3	333.2	350.8
—	68.8	26.8	50.0	−15.0	95.0
1,477.9	2,572.1	2,581.4	2,669.9	2,767.0	3,151.6
85.9	86.4	86.2	90.9	91.3	89.0
17.6	19.8	19.6	22.8	23.1	23.5
68.3	66.6	66.6	68.1	68.2	65.5
15.5	18.1	15.1	13.4	11.9	14.6
14.1	13.6	13.8	9.1	8.7	11.0
19.2	15.3	14.9	10.1	12.0	14.3
20.5	19.8	16.3	14.4	15.2	18.0
1.3	4.5	1.3	4.3	3.2	3.6

TABLE 6.2: (Continued)

	_1970/71_	_1971/72_
Total Resources	3,355.7	3,597.3
GDP at current factor cost	2,820.2	3,047.3
Net indirect taxes	382.4	382.2
GDP at market prices	3,202.6	3,429.5
Exports	447.1	457.2
Imports	600.3	625.0
Total Consumption	2,940.2	3,157.3
Public consumption	821.4	926.1
Private consumption	2,118.8	2,231.2
Gross Domestic Investment	415.5	440.0
Fixed investment	355.5	365.0
Change in stocks	60.0	75.0
Total Expenditures	3,355.7	3,597.3

Share of Main Aggregates in GDP (%)

	_1970/71_	_1971/72_
Total Consumption	91.8	92.1
Public consumption	25.6	27.0
Private consumption	66.2	65.1
Total investment	13.0	12.8
Domestic savings	8.2	7.9
Exports	14.0	13.3
Imports	18.7	18.2
Excess of imports over exports	4.8	4.9

1973	1974	1975	1976	1977
4,003.4	4,702.0	5,834.7	6,565.0	7,765.0
3,464.5	4,111.0	4,779.0	5,455.0	6,483.0
341.8	86.0	82.0	373.0	626.0
3,806.3	4,197.0	4,861.0	5,828.0	7,109.0
532.2	890.0	947.7	1,143.0	1,400.0
729.3	1,395.0	1,920.4	1,880.0	2,056.0
3,503.0	3,972.0	4,506.0	5,160.0	6,050.0
1,074.2	1,101.0	1,213.0	1,361.0	1,590.0
2,428.8	2,871.0	3,293.0	3,799.0	4,460.0
500.4	730.0	1,328.7	1,405.0	1,715.0
462.4	640.0	1,228.7	1,325.0	1,691.0
38.0	90.0	100.0	80.0	124.0
4,003.4	4,702.0	5,834.7	6,565.0	7,765.0
92.0	94.6	92.7	88.5	84.0
28.2	26.2	25.0	23.3	21.0
63.8	68.4	67.7	65.2	63.0
13.1	17.4	27.3	24.1	24.0
8.0	5.4	7.3	11.5	15.0
14.0	21.2	19.5	19.6	20.0
19.1	33.2	39.5	32.3	29.0
5.1	12.0	20.0	12.7	9.0

entrepreneurial initiative generally should help to release substantial amounts of domestic savings. At the same time, sharp increases in income are expected from a number of special sources, as enumerated in the first section of the last chapter. To summarize them here, these special revenue sources are emigrant remittances, petroleum exports, tourism, and Suez Canal revenues, the annual earnings of which all together could jump from the present $4 billion annually to perhaps $13 billion by the mid-1980s.[13] Since the revenues from petroleum exports and the Suez Canal accrue directly to the government, there is a special opportunity for a sharp rise in public savings, which, as a percentage of the GDP, reached 6 percent in 1976. Thus, even with an expected decline in foreign assistance by the 1980s, sufficient capital and foreign exchange should be generated locally to fuel vigorous economic growth and attract significant foreign investor participation.

SKILLS

Although Egypt is better off than most developing countries in the availability of managerial and technical skills, there are still occasional inadequacies in management and in some technical and professional fields.

The present managerial inadequacies are partly a legacy of the Nasser era, when the large-scale nationalizations caused the departure of many foreign and Egyptian managers. Then too, the government domination of so many aspects of the economy during the 1960s stifled entrepreneurial initiative and provided a poor training ground for the development of new managerial talent.[14] The Open Door policy followed since 1973 has as one of its main objectives the creation of a competitive environment so that numerous managers may emerge in the near future. One of the principal current managerial shortcomings concerns the ability to identify promising projects and to carry them through. As a partial measure to remedy this deficiency, the Egypt-U.S. Business Council and the Agency for International Development are cooperating in a project in the period 1978–81 to train 400 middle-level managers in the industrial sector.[15]

Egypt has one of the three best educational systems among developing countries. While the scholastic level is high, there are deficiencies in vocational training. There has been a tendency among talented students to prefer academic over technical education. Again, in the vocational area, there has been a tendency to pursue advanced technology so that there may be an excess supply of high-level technicians and a scarcity of skilled workers. Training programs have been launched to fill these gaps.[16] The Development Industrial Bank provides staff training and technical assistance in project appraisal, while the Engineering and Industrial Design Development Center offers 22 courses taken by some 700 people each year. The National

Academy of Scientific Research and Technology currently supports about 125 research projects. Research is also supported by the following specialized research institutes: the Central Metallurgical Research Institute, the Electronics Industries Research and Development Center, and the Textile Development Center. The National Research Center operates technical training programs in nineteen industrial areas, including metallurgy, glass and ceramics, dyeing and finishing, chemistry, detergents, paints, and dairying. The Agency for International Development finances two initiatives through the National Academy of Science, M.I.T., and Cairo University to expand technical expertise in planning activities and project reviews. Egyptians seek the participation of foreign investors in many projects in order to benefit from the technology and skills they can bring to bear.

The explosion in oil income in Libya and the Arabian peninsula, which was one of the results of the October 1973 war, has had an effect on the availability of skills in Egypt. As mentioned above, lucrative jobs became available in the wealthy Arab states, and many Egyptian professionals and technicians emigrated in response. The 1976 census estimated that 1.43 million Egyptians were abroad on that date, and by 1977, emigrant remittances shot up to $1.5 billion annually. While this capital flow is a welcome assist to Egypt's balance of payments, emigration has caused occasional personnel shortages within Egypt among such tradespersons and professionals as masons, carpenters, electricians, plumbers, doctors, and engineers. While continuing vigorous training programs can fill these gaps in the long run, substantial problems have arisen in the short run. Particularly hard hit has been the construction sector, where costs have been bid up by the shortages in skills and materials. With foreign financial assistance, the Egyptian government is moving forcefully to shore up construction activities.[17]

The establishment of the Arab Organization for Industrialization (AOI) may generate sophisticated skills in a way reminiscent of Mohammed Ali's efforts in the early nineteenth century. AOI was founded in August 1975, with a capital of $1.04 billion put up by Egypt, Saudi Arabia, Qatar, and the United Arab Emirates. AOI is presently producing rockets, bombs, armored vehicles, and automatic weapons and is planning to produce under license American Motors Corporation jeeps, British helicopters and antitank weapons as well as French missiles and jetfighters. The assembly within Egypt of the Alpha-Jet, followed later by the Mirage 2000, is a particularly ambitious project which will involve the dispatch to Egypt of several hundred French engineers and technicians, and will presumably result in new skills being learned by their Egyptian counterparts.

There are thus a number of environmental constraints on significant economic growth in Egypt and on the willingness of many foreign investors to become involved. Substantial progress has already been made on the peace issue and on the supply of adequate capital and skills. The problems represented by bureaucracy and infrastructure are more intractable and will need more time for a resolution. In these areas too, there has been some recent progress, and the Egyptian government appears to be moving forcefully to mitigate some of the major difficulties. On the whole, the environmental factors are rapidly becoming positive, and in the near future there should be continued vigorous economic growth and an attractive climate for the entry into Egypt of numerous foreign investors to participate in a great variety of development projects.

NOTES

1. Many of the American business executives contacted by Arnold McKay cited the uncertain political situation as perhaps the most important constraint on their entering Egypt at that time. See McKay, "U.S. Investment in Egypt May Grow," *Journal of Commerce* (March 29, 1978).

2. This view is corroborated in Egypt-U.S. Business Council, *Report on Foreign Investment in Egypt* (Washington, D.C.: 1976), pp. 4–6.

3. Derogatory comments by some foreign company executives and an extensive analysis of some of the bureaucratic problems appear in ibid., pp. 20–21, 36–38, 45–50, and in Delwin A. Roy, *Private Industry Sector Development in Egypt: An Analysis of Trends 1973–1977*, Report to the Special Task Force Reviewing the U.S. Security Supporting Assistance Program for Egypt (Washington, D.C.: USAID, January 1978), pp. 28–29.

4. Ibid., p. 15, and the above cited pages. In many canvases of people's experience, the negative reactions stand out more sharply than the positive reactions and a distorted overall picture results. The reader should thus observe the cautionary remarks of this Report's author in the foreword, "The study may appear to some as unduly negative but it is not intended to be. It is hoped that the report will provide a better understanding of what the actual problems are and what potential solutions should be pursued . . . The reader must realize that there remain persuasive reasons for investing in Egypt and that the strides made in changing Egypt's political orientation and some of its economic policies . . . have been truly dramatic. Neither Egyptian nor potential foreign investors should be discouraged by our findings."

5. See Arthur D. Little, Inc., *An Assessment of Egypt's Industrial Sector,* Report to the Special Interagency Task Force Reviewing the U.S. Security Supporting Assistance Program for Egypt (Cambridge, MA: January 1978), pp. 104–105, and Roy, op. cit., pp. 30–31, 39.

6. An analysis of a growing loosening-up in bureaucratic controls appears in Little, op. cit., pp. 39–42, 104–105, 116, and Robert E. Driscoll, P. F. Hayek, and Farouk A. Zaki, *Foreign Investment in Egypt: An Analysis of Critical Factors with Emphasis on the Foreign Investment Code* (New York: Fund For Multinational Management Education, 1978), pp. 52–53.

7. The state-owned Nasr Automotive Company is seeking foreign joint venture partners for the assembly or manufacture of cars, engines, tractors, and trucks. Other public-sector companies are apparently seeking foreign partners for the manufacture of lead-acid batteries, refrigerators and stoves, boilers and pressure vessels, and electrical products. See Little, op. cit., p. 117. The Suez Cement Company, which received a loan of $95 million from USAID, was initially capitalized with 80 percent public-sector participation and 20 percent participation by small Egyptian investors. The government has agreed that once the company is in production, the public-sector shares will gradually be sold off to private investors. As reported in Agency for International Development, *U.S. Economic Assistance to Egypt—A Report of a Special Interagency Task Force* (Washington, D.C.: February 15, 1978), p. 17.

8. These indicators come from U.S. government estimates contained in U.S. Department of State—American Embassy, Cairo, *Foreign Economic Trends—Egypt* (Washington, D.C.: August 1978), pp. 6, 13.

9. With telephone facilities so inadequate, many businessmen must make greater use of messengers or make more frequent personal visits. See Egypt-U.S. Business Council, op. cit., pp. 53–54.

10. This analysis of the deficiencies in Egypt's telecommunications facilities is derived from AID, op. cit., pp. 28–29, as well as from the source used there: World Bank, *Arab Republic of Egypt, Economic Management in a Period of Transition* (Washington, D.C.: May 1978), Vol. I., pp. 71–74, and Vol. V, pp. 24–26.

11. Information on Egypt's telecommunications projects has appeared in various issues of the National Foreign Trade Council's *Middle East and North African Notes.*

12. The difficulties underlying low savings rates are well described in Egypt-U.S. Business Council, op. cit. (Appendix II, p. vi), and "Domestic Economic Developments—1976," National Bank of Egypt, *Economic Bulletin* (No. 2, 1977), pp. 129–130, and Little, op. cit., pp. 43–47.

13. These World Bank projections have been labeled optimistic in an AID report. See AID, op. cit., p. 4.

14. Arthur D. Little, Inc., in their op. cit., pp. 68–69, comments that the depletion of managers was most extensive in the upper ranks. Those companies, such as the banks, insurance companies, oil companies, and the Misr Group, that had had thorough training programs, did not do too badly with respect to middle managers.

15. See Driscoll, op. cit., p. 52.

16. A good description of the Egyptian deficiencies in available skills and the recent training and research programs appears in Little, op. cit., pp. 56–61, 105–109, and 126–127.

17. See, for example, AID, op. cit., p. 29. In November 1978, the government of Egypt formulated a $100 million program to establish twenty vocational centers to train construction workers. Equipment is to be obtained from abroad and foreign instructors will be invited to these and other vocational centers, while Egyptian instructors are to be sent abroad.

7

SUMMARY

The analysis made in Chapters 2–6 has concentrated on the various environmental constraints impeding the entry of foreign investors and decreasing their potential contribution to rapid economic growth in Egypt. The basic theme has been that much progress has been made or is in prospect in removing the negative aspects of doing business in Egypt. Before reviewing this material, it would now be well to pinpoint the positive aspects of the foreign investment climate in Egypt. After all, when foreign investors are evaluating a particular country, they wish to ascertain not only how limited the various negative aspects are or may become, but also how extensive are the attractive features.

What constitutes the main attractions for one foreign company may not necessarily be the same for another type of foreign company, although the underlying motive for all companies would appear to be security of investment and high profits. The following checklist of attractive features of the Egyptian investment climate would appear to apply to most foreign companies.[1] 1) The existence of a fairly large domestic market of 40 million persons whose needs for industrial and consumer products are expanding with the rise in their standard of living. 2) A strategic location in a region of tremendous wealth, together with proximity to European, African, and Middle East markets. Access to the European market by manufacturers locating in Egypt was improved by the 1976 trade agreement with the European Economic Community, giving Egyptian industrial products full exemption from EEC customs duties and taxes and seasonal tariff reductions between 40 to 80 percent on Egyptian agricultural products. The very loose Arab Common Market, made up of Egypt, Iraq, Jordan, and Syria, grants some tariff reductions on a reciprocal basis, but much fuller access to the regional Middle East markets is contingent upon a durable peace in the area. 3) Increasing evidence that

Egypt may be on the threshold of rapid self-sustained economic growth, with a burgeoning capacity to absorb investment funds. 4) An abundant labor force with extensive professional and technical skills. The excellent educational facilities continue to turn out young people with high qualifications. 5) The popular endorsement of a major liberalization of government controls, with greater reliance on the market mechanism and private initiative. In response, the private sector is gradually becoming more vigorous. 6) A substantial availability of capital from Egyptian emigrants and Arabian Peninsula investors. 7) The existence of sophisticated industrial and infrastructural facilities, albeit improvements are still desired, particularly in regard to telephones. 8) The availability of foreign exchange and other investment incentives. 9) Pleasant surroundings, including a favorable climate, hospitable people, a low cost of living, and recreation facilities.

PRINCIPAL CONCLUSIONS REACHED ON THE ROLE OF FOREIGN DIRECT INVESTMENT IN PROMOTING RAPID ECONOMIC GROWTH IN EGYPT

The main conclusion reached in this book is that since 1973 there has been a significant improvement in the Egyptian investment climate, in both the legal and general environmental aspects; continuing progress in that area and in achieving self-sustained economic growth promises an increasingly fruitful cooperation between foreign investors and the Egyptian government, banks, and business concerns.

The analysis in Chapter 2 of the three previous growth phases of recent Egyptian economic history constitutes a backdrop to the remainder of the book, which deals with the experience after 1973. A recurring feature of these three phases was the discordance between foreign participation in the Egyptian economy and domestic entrepreneurial activity. During the early growth phase under Mohammed Ali (1816–49), the bootstrap efforts to leapfrog from a rural to a modern industrialized economy failed in the face of foreign hostility. There was then a swift transition to an export-oriented economy during which foreign enterprise was so dominant that Egyptian enterprise stayed largely dormant. During the 1956–73 period, there were vigorous government efforts to promote new industries and build massive irrigation projects, but the pace of progress was meager. With the ascendancy of state paternalism and continual political turmoil, a major suppression of foreign and Egyptian private enterprise took place. The consequent isolation of the Egyptian economy from foreign and domestic sources of creativity stymied general progress. Only during the second growth phase, from about 1920 to the late 1950s, was there some evidence of cooperation and fruitful joint efforts between foreign and Egyptian businessmen. Although there was occasional friction between different groups of businessmen, foreign firms had begun to play a catalytic role in stimulating creative responses by Egyptians in a few sectors.

A turn-around in government attitudes toward foreign investment has taken place in Egypt during the 1970s. As described in Chapter 3, the significant legislative breakthrough occurred in 1974, with the promulgation of a comprehensive foreign investment code. This code contains many new positive features of interest to foreign investors, including liberal provisions on authorized foreign equity, favorable rights on remittance of profits for export-oriented projects, a broad field for foreign investment activity, and the usual incentives and guarantees for free zone projects. A number of legal impediments remained, and the foreign investment community played an active role in the three years of discussion following the 1974 law, as the Egyptian government sought to eliminate many of the remaining ambiguities or difficulties. The result of the discussions was the responsive 1977 amendment. The most important article of that amendment is Article 2 which now uses the same definition of foreign exchange rates for entries and departures of capital. Foreign investors had earlier feared that the murky provision in the 1974 code on the foreign exchange rate could have resulted in large foreign exchange losses upon repatriating capital and remitting profits. Foreign investor concern regarding the right of profit remittances in import substitution projects was partly, but not fully, assuaged by an improved Article 22. Other important new provisions of the 1977 amendment are a clarification that the tax holiday specifically applies to "the general tax on income," a broadening of the specifically allowable investment fields, an enlargement of the exemptions from taxes and duties, and an extension of the code incentives to domestic investments.

The foreign investment climate has been improved by a number of other changes in laws and regulations promulgated from 1974 to 1977. Included have been liberalizations in the foreign exchange regulations, a dismantling of the General Industrial Organizations, greater flexibility in the banking sector, and a strengthening of the role of Egyptian businessmen in importing and in acting as commercial agents for foreign firms. While some foreign investors might feel the need for further legal improvements, the Egyptian government has gone a long way from 1974 to 1977 in addressing the major legal problems. The present legal framework for doing business in Egypt appears to be above average for host developing countries and no longer constitutes a serious obstacle to the entry of foreign investment.

The evolution of a vastly improved legal framework during the 1973–77 period has elicited a large number of approaches to the Egyptian government on the part of foreign investors. These initial approaches had resulted in the approval of 744 projects, all non-petroleum, by the end of 1977, with a proposed foreign equity of £E1.4 billion and an Egyptian equity of £E0.5

billion. While the list of projects approved is fairly impressive, the actual implementation has fallen far short of expectations. Only 161 projects were in operation by the middle of 1977, with a total capitalization outside the petroleum sector of £E240 million.

The most important sectors of interest to foreign investors are banking and petroleum. Aside from these two sectors, the total capital committed to projects in operation is only £E42 million. Tourism and chemicals account for two-thirds of this investment. Descriptive information on foreign investor intentions in the various sectors is presented in Chapter 4 together with some speculation about the reasons for the slow pace of actual implementation. The main reasons appear to be the general recession in the world economy, together with other environmental problems connected with the regional political situation, relationships with the government, infrastructural facilities, capital and foreign exchange availabilities, and skills.

Before analyzing these environmental problems, I present in Chapter 5 the evidence for the claim that there has been much recent economic progress in Egypt. After all, significant economic growth, especially if it becomes self-sustaining, can go a long way toward resolving these environmental constraints. The general economy started to grow strongly during 1975, with the average rate of growth in the gross domestic product shooting above 8 percent during the 1975–77 period. The important factors underlying this acceleration in growth were the reopening of the Suez Canal, the revival of tourism, the surge in emigrant remittances, the rise in petroleum activity, and substantial foreign assistance. Industrial output recovered from the depression it had experienced during the early 1970s and began to make some strides in the mid-1970s, mainly in achieving greater capacity utilization. The major increases have been recorded in chemicals, coal products, basic metals, metallic products, machinery, transport equipment, beverages, and paper. Not much time has elapsed since the commencement of the open-door policy of the Egyptian government, but the attendant revival of private enterprise activity may well bring about a more impressive degree of industrial growth than has been achieved so far.

Despite the vastly improved legal framework for the conduct of business in Egypt, strong foreign investor interest and self-sustained economic growth continue to be handicapped by a number of environmental constraints. As detailed in Chapter 6, substantial progress in resolving these constraints has already been made or is an early prospect. President Sadat's bold peace initiative in November 1977 and the Camp David accords the following year removed political tensions on at least the Sinai front. The modest success of these negotiations marked an improvement in the regional political situation and has thus assuaged some of the political uncertainties of foreign businessmen. The difficult dealings which some foreign investors have had with the government have been a more intractable constraint, since institutional behavior takes time to change. There have been complaints of occasional dilatory handling of investment applications as well as a tendency among some working level Egyptian officials to apply precedents from the pre-liberalization era in the numerous areas of ambiguity. This slow handling and the differences in basic governmental attitudes toward foreign investors have sometimes bred in the latter a general atmosphere of low confidence in Egyptian decision-making. Some progress has been made since about 1975 in loosening up bureaucratic controls through a reduction in the number of steps in the approval process, the reorganization at the General Authority for Foreign Investment, and regulations strengthening the authority of private managers. Further liberalization of government controls is expected; thus, the relationships between foreign businessmen and Egyptian government officials, which have already improved over the last few years, should become increasingly productive.

Serious dissatisfaction exists with Egyptian performance connected with port facilities, railways, power distribution, and, most particularly, telecommunications. These inadequacies have been due to insufficient investments made in the past, combined with low user fees. Investments in the infrastructural sector are now rising steeply, especially to resolve the most urgent problems; thus, foreign investor dissatisfaction with some infrastructural deficiencies may be removed during the next several years.

The other two environmental constraints on rapid economic growth and serious foreign-investor interest have been availabilities of capital and skills. Substantial progress was made during 1976 and 1977 in increasing the domestic mobilization of investment funds, and several special revenue sources give an ever higher yield, so there will be little worry on this score during the 1980s. Emigration has caused temporary shortages in certain skills, but the excellence of the general Egyptian educational system and the current special training programs promise to fill the few gaps in special skills.

On the whole, the legal framework has become satisfactory and the environmental factors are rapidly becoming positive and will attract numerous foreign investors, who in the process will help to promote rapid economic growth in Egypt. An outline of future economic growth and some of the possible opportunities for foreign business participation therein are presented in the final section of this book.

A POSSIBLE OUTLINE OF FUTURE ECONOMIC GROWTH AND FOREIGN BUSINESS PARTICIPATION

Egypt made its first comprehensive effort at detailed planning for the period 1960–65. Bad harvests, the effects of the Yemen and 1967 wars, and frictions within the Egyptian political and economic system torpedoed this first planning effort, and planning largely gave way to concentration on immediate problems. Egyptian government officials renewed their efforts after the October 1973 war, with the formulation of a "1976–80" plan, followed by the currently effective 1978–82 plan. There are now indications that Egyptian officials are adopting the "rolling plan" concept, that is, with the passage of each year, the terminal year of the plan will be deferred. Appropriate adjustments to the objectives and targets of the plan will then be made in the light of changing circumstances.

Egyptian planning with respect to the individual sector targets or growth rates can be classified as optimistic expectations. Everything would have to work out very well indeed for the aggregate objectives and most of the sector targets to be realized.

The 1978–82 Plan contains the central projection of an average annual rate of increase in real terms in the gross domestic product of an astounding 12 percent. GDP is scheduled to go from an estimated £E6.6 billion in 1978 to £E10.4 billion in 1982, both in 1977 prices.[2] To achieve this objective, Egyptian planners assume a real rate of increase for total investment of 13 percent per year, and for exports of nearly 17 percent per year. An incremental capital-output ratio of 2.5 is also assumed. This unusual efficiency in investment is expected to be brought about by giving high priority to completing ongoing projects and to adding facilities to old projects on a complementary basis in order to eliminate idle capacity. Other general priorities are export orientation and projects with important external linkages, such as fertilizers and building materials.

An indication of sectoral priorities is given in Table 7.1, which presents a breakdown of investment intentions by sector. The major sector to receive investment funds is transportation and communications, (27.3 percent including the Suez Canal). Next in priority is the field of industry and mining, which is to receive 24 percent of the predicted investment funds.

In agriculture, there is to be increased mechanization, as a way of using land resources more efficiently and also in order to take advantage of ready sources of meat. There is to be a downgrading in cotton, with production planned to fall to 800,000 tons annually, and a corresponding increase in acreage for cereal grains, fruits, and vegetables.[3] In housing, the main emphasis is on the creation of new urban centers to act as new poles of development and to relieve the pressures on the existing crowded cities. In other infrastructural services, attention is being given to renovate and upgrade existing facilities and to take initial steps to expand them to catch up with burgeoning demand.

The ambitious character of the 1978–82 Plan is most notable in industry where, as is shown in Table 7.2, the annual average of industrial investment is scheduled to rise from £E292 million during the 1975–77 period to £E682 million during the Plan period.[4] This is certainly a sharp rise, although there

TABLE 7.1: Planned Investment, 1978–82 (1977 prices)

Area of Investment	1978	1982	1978–82	Percent of Public Investment 1978–82
		£E Million		
	1,584.1	2,350.3	10,175.4	100.0
Agriculture	65.4	91.1	395.7	3.9
Irrigation and drainage	93.8	102.4	483.2	4.7
Industry and metallurgy	344.1	633.3	2,412.6	23.7
Petroleum	75.0	149.0	562.4	5.5
Electricity	122.6	193.7	924.0	9.1
Construction	32.0	48.4	213.8	2.1
Transportation and communications	370.5	528.5	2,307.3	22.6
Suez Canal	119.0	32.0	474.8	4.7
Commerce and finance	30.7	50.5	215.8	2.2
Housing	85.0	134.6	585.0	5.8
Utilities	94.6	135.0	622.8	6.1
Services	158.5	221.8	978.0	9.6
Private	176.0	500.0	1,458.0	
Total	1,760.1	2,850.3	11,633.4	

Source: Ministry of Planning, 1978–82 Plan, Vol. 1.

TABLE 7.2: Distribution of Industrial Investment by Responsible Ministry, 1975–77 and 1978–82 (£E million, 1975 prices)

Sector	1975	1976	1977*	1978–82
Industry	202	229	171	1,872
Military production	25	29	19	168
Supply	5	12	10	92
Housing and reconstruction	9	34	46	394
Public Sector	256	317	277	2,702
Private Sector	—	13	13	709
Total	256	330	290	3,411

*Estimated
Source: Ministry of Planning, 1978–82 Plan, Vol. 6.

appears to be a distortion in the omission of much private-sector expenditure for industrial investment in the 1975–77 period. (Compare rows three and fourteen of Table 6.1 and the final row of Table 4.5.) Turning to the sectoral distribution of industrial investments and, leaving aside the controversial Abu Thartur phosphate project, there seems to be a remarkably even division of investment allocations. As is shown in Table 7.3, roughly £E240 million is

TABLE 7.3: Investment in Industry by Principal Sector, 1975–77 and Projected 1978–82 (£E million, 1975 prices)

Industrial Sector	1975–77	During Plan
Food	85.2	252.2
Textiles	132.6	236.6
Chemicals	168.0	231.1
Metals	37.1	241.0
Iron and steel complex	359.8	529.8*
Engineering and electrical	48.2	247.7
Mining	37.4	90.1
TOTAL	881.7	1,872.2

*Abu Thartur, not yet demonstrated to be economically feasible, accounts for 28 percent of total projected investment in industry. The project has a high infrastructure and mining content.

Source: Ministry of Planning, 1978–82 Plan, Vol. 6.

planned to be invested in each of five industrial sectors: food, textiles, chemicals, metals, and engineering and electrical. In keeping with the emphasis noted above in the overall plan on existing projects, nearly 60 percent by value of the industrial investments within the purview of the Ministry of Industry is scheduled to be allocated for the completion of ongoing projects or for refurbishing or replacing existing equipment.[5]

The total industrial output is scheduled to rise from about £E3.8 billion in 1977 to £E6.1 billion in 1982. In regard to public-sector firms under the jurisdiction of the Ministry of Industry alone, output is to rise from nearly £E2 billion to £E3 billion. By sector, the average annual rates of increase are anticipated as follows: food—6 percent, textiles—10 percent, chemicals—18 percent, engineering and metals—26 percent, and mining—28 percent.[6] These targeted rates of output imply considerable success at efforts to diversify Egypt's industrial structure. As noted in Chapter 5, however, progress so far in promoting greater industrial sophistication has not been impressive, and 1982 may still be too early to have had such rapid rates of increase in the production of advanced industrial products.

The aggregate objectives of the Egyptian government for rates of increase in GDP, investment, export, productivity, and industrial output are far beyond historical experience and as such are not likely to be realized, at least by 1982. There have, of course, been examples of such high growth rates in other countries, as in Japan during the 1960s and in South Korea during the 1970s. In these countries, however, there has been a much greater historical buildup of the necessary skills and behavioral traits and a closer community of interest among the different social groups than is the case in Egypt. There is no harm in striving for high objectives so long as it encourages the taking of related useful steps and stimulates greater than normal progress. The achievements actually realized by a certain date are then likely to be greater than if lower targets are sought. Full attainment of the more lofty objectives might then come about, after a delay of several years, through a detailed analysis of the reasons for currently falling short and a determined effort at persuading the various groups to cooperate diligently in taking the necessary remedial actions.

The public sector continues to be the principal instrument of development, with public investment anticipated to total nearly 88 percent of the total. Public investments will also predominate in industry in view of the great importance attached to the completion or rehabilitation of existing projects or facilities. When we turn to the initiation of new industrial projects for new plants or significant expansions, we find a major reliance on private Egyptian and foreign investment. In fact, except for the defense area and a couple of basic industries such as steel, most new industrial projects are expected to be realized through private firms alone or through private firms in joint ventures with public-sector companies. The participation of foreign investors is considered a precondition for the implementation of such ventures because of the imported technology which is urgently needed for efficiency in operations or for turning out high-quality products.

As a follow-up to the industrial projections made in the 1978–82 Plan, the General Organization for Industrialization has carried out six sectoral studies to identify attractive investment possibilities.[7] The projects listed below are considered by the Egyptian government to be prime candidates for the participation of Egyptian and foreign private investors. In some cases, the appropriate vehicle may be a joint venture between foreign investors and a public-sector company. These possible investment opportunities are:

Food

- Wet milling facility for corn syrups
- Three edible oil plants
- Two animal feed plants
- A yeast plant

Textiles

- Renovation of a jute mill
- A new polyester cotton spinning mill
- Two new cotton weaving mills

Pulp and paper

- A bagasse newsprint facility attached to a sugar mill
- Five printing and writing paper plants

- A pulp mill
- A corrugated linerboard plant
- A duplex and multiple board plant
- A tissue mill
- A wastepaper mill
- Cigarette paper

Building Materials

- Additions to cement plants
- Additions or new plants for asbestos pipes, asbestos sheets, concrete pipes and poles, clay pipes, and floor tiles
- New brick plants
- A plant for flat glass and another for glass wool and fiber glass
- A plant for spiral welded steel

Metallurgy

- A copper rod casting plant

Engineering

- New facilities for railway and streetcar coaches
- Diesel engine plants
- Television production
- Manufacture of handling equipment
- Production of a broader range of machine tools
- Expanded output of trucks, buses, and tractors
- Manufacture of electric motors, generators, and larger-size boilers
- Expanded production of wet and dry batteries

There are, in fact, numerous investment opportunities in Egypt besides the ones uncovered in the GOFI sectoral studies. These opportunities exist in agriculture, tourism, and infrastructural facilities as well as in other industrial sectors. As long as Egypt succeeds in its efforts to promote rapid self-sustaining economic growth and, in so doing, removes the remaining environmental constraints discussed in this book, there should be an increasing range of opportunities for fruitful cooperation between foreign investors and Egyptian public bodies and private firms.

NOTES

1. A good digest of the attractive features of the Egyptian investment climate appears in Robert E. Driscoll, P. F. Hayek, Farouk A. Zaki, *Foreign Investment in Egypt: An Analysis of*

Critical Factors with Emphasis on the Foreign Investment Code (New York: Fund for Multinational Management Education, 1978), pp. 21–24.

2. The prediction of a 12 percent growth rate in the Gross Domestic Product over the five years, together with the predicted GDP figure for 1982, appears in Ministry of Planning, Government of Egypt, *Draft Five Year Plan, 1978–82* (Cairo, 1977), Vol. 1, Table 5.

3. The objectives in agriculture are presented in ibid., Vol. 4.

4. A brief discussion of the allocation of industrial investments according to the government ministry in charge appears in Arthur D. Little, Inc., *An Assessment of Egypt's Industrial Sector,* Report to the Special Interagency Task Force Reviewing the U.S. Security Supporting Assistance Program for Egypt (Cambridge, MA, January 1978), pp. 85–86. The major industrial responsibility of the Ministry of Housing and Reconstruction is cement.

5. A table in ibid., p. 88, shows that of £E1.9 billion in industrial investments scheduled to come within the purview of the Ministry of Industry during 1978–82, £E824 million is for ongoing projects, £E198 million for refurbishing and replacement, £E349 million for joint ventures, and £E477 million for other new projects.

6. These targeted rates of increase in industrial output are Egyptian government projections appearing in ibid., pp.91–93.

7. These sectoral studies were financed by the World Bank for the General Organization for Industrialization. The studies are reviewed in ibid., pp. 117–120, and in Appendix A-1 through A-52.

APPENDIX

THE ARAB REPUBLIC OF EGYPT

The General Authority for Investment and Free Zones

LAW NO. 43 OF 1974 CONCERNING THE INVESTMENT OF ARAB AND FOREIGN FUNDS AND THE FREE ZONES AS AMENDED BY LAW NO. 32 OF 1977

1977

Decree of the President of the Arab Republic of Egypt enacting Law No. 43 of 1974, concerning Arab and Foreign Capital Investment and Free Zones.

In The Name Of The People

The President Of The Republic

The People's Assembly has approved the following law, and it has been issued:

Art. 1.   Arab and foreign investments and free zones are governed by the attached law.

Art. 2.   Matters not covered by this Law are subject to the applicable laws and regulations.

Art. 3.   **The Minister of Economy and Economic Cooperation shall issue, upon recommendation of the Board of Directors of the General Authority for Investment and the Free Zones, the executive regulations implementing this law within three months of its enactment.**

Law No. 43 of 1974 has been amended by Law No. 32 of 1977 (the "Amending Law"). The following text of Law No. 43 incorporates all changes made by Articles 1–4 of the Amending Law, which changes are set forth in bold type. Articles 5, 6, 7 and 8 of the Amending Law do not effect changes in the text of Law 43 and are set forth in Annex A hereto.

This text is in accordance with the official version appearing in National Bank of Egypt, *Economic Bulletin,* No. 2, 1977.

Art. 4.   Law No. 65 of 1971 on Arab Capital Investment and Free Zones is hereby repealed. Any other provision contrary to what is stated in the present law is also repealed. Projects approved under said law shall continue to enjoy the rights and privileges specified thereunder. Projects approved prior to the implementation of Law No. 65 of 1971 shall continue to enjoy the privileges and guarantees granted to such projects prior to the coming into force of said law.

Art. 5.   This Law shall be published in the Official Gazette and will receive the seal of the State and shall come into force from the date of its publication.

Signature of the President
19 June, 1974.

CHAPTER ONE

Investment of Arab and Foreign Capital

Art. 1.   The term "Project" in the application of the provisions of this Law shall mean any activity included within any of the spheres therein specified and approved by the Board of Directors of the General Authority **for Investment and Free Zones.**

Art. 2.   The term "Invested Capital" in the application of the provisions of this Law shall be deemed to mean the following: i) Free foreign currency duly transferred to the Arab Republic of Egypt through a bank registered at the Central Bank of Egypt for utilization in the execution or expansion of a project. ii) Machinery, equipment, transportation equipment, raw materials and commodity requirements imported from abroad and necessary for the establishment or expansion of the project, provided that such are compatible with modern technological developments and have not been previously used, unless the Authority's Board of Directors grants exemption from such condition. iii) Intangible assets, such as patents and trade marks registered with member states of the International Convention for the Protection of Industrial Property, or in accordance with the rules of international registration contained in the international conventions concluded in this respect and held by residents abroad and pertaining to the projects. iv) The free foreign currency spent on preliminary studies, research, and incorporation and assumed by the investor within the limits approved by the Authority's Board of Directors. v) Profits realized by the project if utilized in increasing its capital or if invested in another project, conditional on the approval of the Authority's Board of

Directors in both cases. vi) The free foreign currency transferred to the Arab Republic of Egypt through a bank registered at the Central Bank of Egypt and utilized to subscribe to Egyptian stock or to purchase same from the stock exchange in the Arab Republic of Egypt in accordance with the rules adopted by the Authority's Board of Directors. vii) The free foreign currency transferred to the Arab Republic of Egypt through a bank registered at the Central Bank of Egypt and utilized in purchasing land whether vacant or not, for the construction of buildings thereon pursuant to the provisions of this Law, even if purchased before obtaining the Board of Directors' approval as long as the act of purchase was effected according to the prevailing Laws and on a date subsequent to the entering into force of Law No. 65 of 1971.

The valuation of the invested capital referred to in items 2, 3 and 4 shall be subject to the approval of the Authority's Board of Directors and shall be made in accordance with the rules and procedures which shall be specified in the executive regulations.

Art. 2 bis. **Invested capital shall be transferred to, and exported from, the Arab Republic of Egypt, and profits generated therefrom shall be transferred in foreign currency abroad in accordance with the provisions of this Law, at the highest rate prevailing and declared for free foreign currency by the competent Egyptian authorities.**

The provisions of the preceding paragraph shall apply to land and property that represent an integral part of the capital assets of the projects approved by the General Authority for Investment and the Free Zones.

Art. 3. The investment of Arab and Foreign capital in the Arab Republic of Egypt shall be for the purpose of realising the objectives of economic and social development within the framework of the State's general policy and national plan, provided that the investment is made in projects in need of international expertise in the spheres of modern development or in projects requiring foreign capital. The projects, contained in the lists to be prepared by the Authority and approved by the Council of Ministers, shall be in the following fields: i) Industrialization, mining, energy, tourism, transportation, and other fields. ii) Reclamation of barren land and cultivation thereof under long-term tenancy not exceeding 50 years, with a possible renewal on the proposal of the Authority and approval of the Council of Ministers for an additional 50 years, and projects for developing animal production and water wealth. iii) Projects for housing and for urban development, by which is meant investment in the division of land into parcels and the construction of new buildings together with the public utilities connected therewith.

The purchase of a building already in existence or of vacant land is not to be deemed to be a "project" in the context of the provisions of this Law unless intended for construction or for rebuilding and not for the purpose of resale in order to benefit from an increase in market value, without prejudice however to the regulations governing the disposal and re-export of invested capital contained in this Law. The building has to be completed within the period specified by the Authority's Board of Directors, with no obligation on the part of the State to vacate such real property. iv) Investment companies which aim at utilizing funds in the fields enumerated in this Law. v) Investment banks and merchant banks and reinsurance companies whose activities shall be confined to transactions effected in free currencies. The aforementioned banks and companies are entitled to directly undertake financing and investment operations, whether they are in projects in the free zones or for local, joint or foreign projects established within the Arab Republic of Egypt. They may also finance Egyptian foreign trade transactions. vi) Banks engaging in local currency transactions, so long as they are in the form of joint ventures in which local Egyptian capital holds at least 51%. **vii) Construction activities in regions outside the agricultural area and the perimeters of existing cities. viii) Construction contracting activities undertaken by Joint Stock Companies in which there is a 50% minimum Egyptian capital participation. ix) Technical consultant activities in the form of Joint Stock Companies in partnership with foreign international consultant firms subject to their being related to any projects in the project areas mentioned herein, their activity being essential to the project and to the approval of the Authority's Board of Directors. Each operation is to have a special account in conformity with the system defined by the Minister of Economy and Economic Cooperation and approved by the Board of Directors of the Authority.**

Special priority shall be given to those projects which are designed to generate exports, encourage tourism, or reduce the need to import basic commodities, as well as to projects which require advanced technical expertise or which make use of patents or trade marks of worldwide reputation.

Art. 4. The capital invested in the Arab Republic of Egypt under the provisions of this Law shall take the form of participation with public or private Egyptian capital in such fields and under such terms and conditions as are set forth in Articles 2 and 3 of the present law. By way of exception from the above: a) Housing projects, constructed for the purpose of investment, may be undertaken only by Arab capital; foreign capital may not undertake housing projects even in participation with Egyptian capital.

The term "Arab invested capital" shall mean such capital as is owned by a natural person having the nationality of an Arab country, or a juridical person, provided that the majority of its capital shall be held by citizens of one or more Arab countries. b) Arab or foreign capital may not operate without local participation in investment banks and merchant banks whose activities are confined to transactions effected in free currencies so long as they take the form of branches of firms the principal offices of which are situated abroad. c) The Authority's Board of Directors, by a two thirds majority vote of its members, may approve the investment of Arab or foreign capital without local participation in the other fields specified in Article 3.

Art. 5.   Real estate may not be expropriated for the purpose of building investment projects unless such is deemed to be a public utility pursuant to the Law.

Art. 6.   Irrespective of the nationality or domicile of their owners, projects in the Arab Republic of Egypt approved under the provisions of this Law shall enjoy the guarantees and privileges set forth in this Law.

Subject to the Authority's approval according to its rules and regulations, projects established in any area of the areas set forth in Article 3 entirely with Egyptian capital and owned by Egyptian nationals shall enjoy the privileges and exemptions set forth in Articles 9, 14, 15, 16, 17 and 18.

Subject to the Authority's approval, such exemptions shall apply to Joint Stock companies existing at the time of the enactment of this law within the limit of new expansion in fields approved in the Law through an increase in capital by cash subscription.

Art. 7.   Projects may not be nationalized or confiscated.

The assets of such projects cannot be seized, blocked, confiscated or sequestrated except by judicial procedures.

Art. 8.   Investment disputes in respect of the implementation of the provisions of this Law shall be settled in a manner to be agreed upon with the investor, or within the framework of the agreements in force between the Arab Republic of Egypt and the investor's home country, or within the framework of the Convention for the Settlement of Investment Disputes between the State and the nationals of other countries to which Egypt has adhered by virtue of Law No. 90 of 1971, where such Law applies.

Disputes may be settled through arbitration. An Arbitration Board shall be constituted, comprising a member on behalf of each disputing party and a third member acting as chairman to be jointly named by the said two members. Failing agreement on the nomination of the third member within thirty days of the appointment of the second member, the chairman shall be chosen, at the request of either party, by the Supreme Council of Judicial Bodies from among counsellors of the judiciary in the Arab Republic of Egypt.

The Arbitration Board shall lay down its rules of procedure unrestricted by the rules contained in the Civil and Commercial Code of Procedures, save the rules which relate to the basic guarantees and principles of litigation. The Board shall see to it that the dispute is expediently resolved. Awards shall be rendered by majority vote and shall be final and binding on both parties and enforceable as any other final judgment.

The Arbitration Board shall decide on the costs of Arbitration and shall determine who shall bear such costs.

Art. 9.　　Companies enjoying the provisions of this Law shall be deemed to belong to the private sector of the economy, irrespective of the legal nature of the indigenous capital participating therein. Legislation, regulations, and statutes applicable to the public sector of the economy and its employees shall not apply to said companies.

Art. 10.　　Projects enjoying the provisions of this Law shall not be subject to Law No. 73 of 1973, in connection with the conditions and procedures for electing labor representatives to the Board of Directors of Public sector organizations, joint stock companies, and private associations and establishments.

The statutes of the company shall show the method to be applied for labor participation in the management of the project.

Art. 11.　　Provisions applicable to laborers and employees provided for in Law No. 26 for the year 1954, concerning certain provisions on Joint Stock Companies, Partnerships and Limited Liability Companies, shall apply to the projects irrespective of their legal form. The employees of said projects shall be subject to the Social Insurance Law unless the project provides a better insurance scheme approved by the General Organization for Social Insurance.

Employees of projects shall be exempted from the provisions of Law No. 113 of 1958, and Article 21 of the Labor Law No. 91 of 1959. Employees and members of Boards of Directors of projects shall also be exempted from the provisions of Law No. 113 of 1961, limiting the remuneration of the chairman and members of Boards of Directors or seconded members to a maximum of £E 5000.

Art. 11 (bis).　　**The projects referred to in the first paragraph of the previous article are subject to the restrictions pertaining to employees of Government and representative bodies set forth in Articles 95 to 98 of Law No. 26 of 1954, and to the prohibitions set forth in Article 28 of Law No. 38 of 1972, with regard to members of the People's Assembly.**

Prohibited activities in accordance with the provisions referred to in the previous article include undertaking any private activity, directly or through an intermediary, including consultant activities, if during the

year prior to leaving office or employment, the Minister or public official was involved in licensing the establishment of these projects or supervising their activity.

In the application of the provisions of this Law, the term "Minister" shall refer to the Prime Minister, Deputy Prime Ministers, Ministers and Deputy Ministers.

Art. 12. Companies enjoying the provisions of this Law shall be exempted from the provisions of Article 14 paragraph 5, of Law No. 26 of 1954, concerning certain provisions on Joint Stock Companies, Partnerships and Companies with Limited Liability, provided a percentage of the net profits of such companies is to be distributed annually among employees and labor in accordance with the rules proposed by the Company's Board of Directors and approved by the General Assembly.

These companies shall also be exempted from the provisions of Article 2 paragraph (1), **Article 11, Article 15 paragraph (1),** Article 21 paragraphs (1) and (4), **Article 24 paragraph (2), Articles 28, 30, 33 and 33 (bis),** Article 41 paragraph (4), **Article 66 paragraph (1) of Law No. 26 of 1954.** Representatives of foreign natural or juridical persons shall be exempted from the provisions of Article 29 of such Law and non Egyptian individuals shall be exempt from Article 31 thereof. **Shares, including founders' shares, may not be transferred during the first two years of the project unless approved by the Board of Directors of the Authority. These companies shall also be exempted from the provisions of Law No. 137 of 1961, concerning the formation of Boards of Directors of Joint Stock Companies.**

Art. 13. Without prejudice to the provisions of item 6 of Article 3, the banks benefiting from the provisions of this law shall be excepted from the requirement that Egyptians should own all of its shares contained in paragraph (a) of Article 21 of the Law on Banks and Credit issued by Law No. 163 for 1957. Said banks shall also be excepted from paragraph (c) of the same article.

Likewise, investment and merchant banks and reinsurance companies, referred to in Article 3, paragraph 5, hereof, shall be exempted from the provisions of the laws, regulations, and resolutions regulating control of exchange transactions.

Art. 14. By way of exception from the provisions of **Law No. 97 of 1976,** regulating transactions in foreign currency, projects shall have the right to maintain a foreign currency account or accounts with banks registered at the Central Bank of Egypt in the Arab Republic of Egypt. On the credit side of such account or accounts shall be entered the balance of the capital paid in foreign currencies, **loans and any other funds of the project so long as they shall be in free currencies, funds purchased by the project from local banks at the highest rate prevailing and declared for foreign currency,** the proceeds of the visible and invisible exports of the enterprise **and the proceeds of sales to the local market in foreign currency.**

The project shall have the right without special permit or authorization, to utilize the said account in transferring the amounts authorized under the provisions of this Law for payments for imports of commodities and investment goods necessary for the operation of the project, for meeting invisible expenses in connection with such imports, for the payment of interest and principal on foreign **currency** loans, for settling any other expenses necessary for the project, **and for purchases of local currency at the highest rate prevailing and declared for foreign currency.** The project shall undertake to submit to the Authority, **at the end of each fiscal year,** a statement indicating the movement in this account, together with such documents and details as the Authority may request to ascertain that the utilization has been in compliance with the purposes set forth in this Law. **The statement shall be certified by a certified public accountant.**

Art. 15.   By way of exception from the provisions of the laws, regulations, and resolutions governing imports, enterprises enjoying the provisions of this Law shall be allowed to import, on condition of inspection but without a license, whether by themselves or through a third party, the production facilities, material, machinery, equipment, spare parts, and transportation equipment required for the installation and operation of the project, that are compatible with the nature of their activities. Such operations shall be excepted from the procedure requiring submission to a committee for the purpose of selecting the best tender, but there shall be no obligation on the part of the Government to provide the foreign currency necessary for the importing operations beyond the bank accounts mentioned in the preceding Article.

Projects shall be authorized to export their products whether by themselves or through an intermediary without a license, and without such projects having to be registered in the Registry of Exporters.

Art. 16.   Without prejudice to more favourable tax exemptions provided for in any other law, projects shall be exempted from the tax on commercial and industrial profits and the taxes appendent thereto; likewise the profits distributed shall be exempted from the tax on the revenues from moveable capital and the taxes appendent thereto, **and, as the case may be, from the tax on commercial and industrial profits and the taxes appendent thereto, as well as from the general tax on income, relative to the taxable proportion of such profits as set forth in this provision,** such exemption to be for a period of five years from the first **fiscal** year following commence-ment of production or engagement in activities, as the case may be. Such exemptions shall apply for the same period to the proceeds of the profits which are reinvested in the enterprise **and for special reserves that are debited to the distribution account after deduction of net profits and allocated to consolidate the company's financial position and undis-tributed profits earned during the exemption period and distributed after such period has elapsed.** The shares shall be exempted from the annual proportional stamp duty for five years following the date duties are legally due for the first time.

The exemption from the general tax on income is conditioned upon such income not being subject to similar taxation in the investor's home country or in the country to which income is transferred, as the case may be.

On the proposal of the Authority's Board of Directors, with the approval of the Council of Ministers, the period of exemption shall be eight years, provided such period is required by consideration of public interest in view of the nature of the project, its geographical location, its importance to economic development, the volume of its capital, and the extent to which it participates in exploiting natural resources and increasing exports.

Exemptions for projects involving reconstruction, establishment of new cities outside the agricultural area and the perimeters of existing cities, and land reclamation shall be for a ten year period that may be extended to fifteen years with the approval of the President of the Republic upon recommendation of the Authority's Board of Directors.

Also, with the approval of the President of the Republic, upon recom-mendation of the Authority's Board of Directors, all capital assets and im-ported construction material and **components** necessary for **founding** projects approved under this Law may be exempted from, **or granted the privileges of deferred payment or installment payments for, all or part of** the customs duties and any other taxes or dues **provided that, in the case of exemption, if such items are locally disposed of within five years from the date of import, all such taxes and duties previously exempted shall be paid. In the case of deferred or installment payments, if such items are locally disposed of within five years, or within the deferred or install-ment payments period if such period exceeds five years, all such taxes and duties shall be paid.**

Art. 17. **After the expiration of the tax exemption period established under Article 16, and without prejudice to the provisions of such Article,** the profits distributed by a project shall be exempted from the general tax on income up to a maximum of 5% **of the original amount** of the taxpayer's share in the invested capital.

Art. 18.   Interest due on loans in foreign **currency** concluded by the project even if in the form of a deposit shall be exempted from all taxes and dues. Such exemptions shall apply as well to the interest on foreign **currency** loans concluded by the Egyptian participant to finance his share in the project.

Art. 19.   Buildings utilized for administrative purposes, and above the average housing, constructed under the provisions of this Law shall not be subject to the rules limiting rents as stipulated in the laws governing rental of premises.

Art. 20.   Foreign experts and employees brought from abroad to work in any of the projects enjoying the provisions of this Law shall be permitted to transfer from Egypt a portion of the wages, salaries, and compensations which they receive in the Republic of Egypt, provided the percentage shall not exceed fifty percent of their gross earnings.

All payments subject to the Employment Earnings tax, such as wages, salaries, bonuses or other similar payments made to foreign employees by projects established according to the provisions of this Law shall be exempt from the General Tax on Income.

Art. 21.   The party concerned may request the re-exportation or disposal of the invested capital after obtaining the approval of the Authority's Board of Directors, provided that five years shall have elapsed from the date of importation of the capital fixed in the registration certificate (the Authority's Board of Directors may waive this condition if it is evident that the accepted project, for which funds have been transferred, cannot be implemented or continued for reasons beyond the control of the investor or for other exceptional circumstances to be considered by the Authority's Board of Directors) in accordance with the following: i) Invested capital may be transferred abroad at the **highest rate prevailing and declared for foreign currency in five equal annual installments.** By way of exception, the invested capital, calculated under the provisions of this article, shall be transferrable in full **to the extent of the credit balance in the foreign exchange account referred to in Article 14 or** if the investors had disposed **of such invested capital in exchange for free foreign** currency, **provided that the Authority is notified of this action. ii) If the invested capital was brought in kind, it may, with the approval of the Authority's Board of Directors, be re-exported in kind. iii) The invested capital registered with the Authority may be disposed of for free foreign currency after informing the Authority. Nevertheless the investor may with the approval of the Authority's Board of Directors dispose of his funds as registered with the Authority or dispose of part thereof in favor of another party in local currency in** which case the party in favor of which such disposal has taken place shall not enjoy the right to transfer set forth in this Law. In both cases, however, the party in favor of which such transfer has taken place shall replace the original investor in enjoying the provisions of this Law.

Shares offered in free foreign currency may in all cases be sold at the Egyptian Stock Exchange in which case the proceeds of sales shall be transferable to the seller's account abroad.

Art. 22. The Authority's approval of a project shall include specifying the rules for transferring the return on invested capital abroad, if so requested by the investor, in accordance with the following: i) Projects realizing self sufficiency in their foreign currency needs, whose earnings from visible exports cover all their requirements of imports of machinery, equipment, production inputs and materials, and pay for all foreign currency loans and interest thereon, shall be permitted to transfer their annual net profits **determined at the highest rate prevailing and declared for foreign currency within the limits of the credit balance of the foreign currency account authorized by the provisions of Article 14 of this Law. ii) Projects that are basically not export oriented, and that limit the country's need for imports, shall be permitted to transfer, in whole or in part, their net profits at the highest rate prevailing and declared for foreign currency within the limits approved by the Authority and subject to the currency regulations in force.** iii) Net revenue on housing, the rentals of which are paid in free foreign currency, shall be transferable in full. Net revenue on housing the rentals of which are payable in local currency shall be transferable up to **8%** per annum of invested capital. Popular housing, and housing in new cities and outside the agricultural areas and the perimeters of existing cities shall be allowed to transfer net revenues up to **14%** of invested capital. Reinvestment of revenue not transferable shall be permitted within an additional **8%** per annum of invested capital, and the funds reinvested under this provision in approved fields shall be considered as invested capital in the sense of the provisions of this Law.

CHAPTER TWO

Joint Ventures

Art. 23. Joint ventures established under the provisions of this Law in the form of joint stock or limited liability companies shall specify in their Articles of Incorporation the names of their respective contracting parties, the legal form of the company, its name, purpose of activities, duration, capital, percentage of participation by Egyptian, Arab, and foreign parties, and methods of subscriptions.

Statutes of the company shall be patterned after the model adopted by resolution of the Council of Ministers on the basis of a proposal by the Board of Directors of the General Authority for Investment and Free Zones, taking into consideration the privileges, guarantees, and exemptions laid down in this Law.

In all joint ventures the General Authority for Investment and Free Zones shall have sole competence to review and approve, in compliance with the provisions of the present law, the Articles of Incorporation.

The signatures of all partners or shareholders on contracts relating to all projects whatever their legal status shall be endorsed against an Endorsement Fee of one quarter of one percent of the capital of the project to a maximum not exceeding one thousand Egyptian pounds (£E 1000) or its equivalent in foreign currency, as the case may be, whether such endorsement be carried out in Egypt or at an Egyptian representational office abroad. Contracts establishing a project and all contracts relating to a project including loan agreements, mortgages, purchases of real estate and machinery, construction contracting and other contracts shall be exempt from stamp duties, registration and publication fees until one year following the commencement of operations.

This provision shall also apply to projects extablished in the Free Zone.

Art. 24.   The statutes of joint stock companies formed under the provisions of this Law shall be promulgated by decree of the President of the Republic. Such companies shall enjoy a juridical personality as from the date of publication of their statutes and Articles of Incorporation pursuant to the Executive Regulations of this Law. The foregoing provisions shall apply to any amendment of the company's statutes.

CHAPTER THREE

General Authority for Arab and Foreign Investment and Free Zones

Art. 25.   A General Authority, **whose Board of Directors shall be under the Chairmanship of the Minister of Economy and Economic Cooperation shall be created with the name "The General Authority for Investment and Free Zones"** (herein referred to in this Law as "the Authority").

Its principal offices shall be in the city of Cairo and it may maintain offices outside the Arab Republic of Egypt.

The Authority shall enjoy juridical personality, and shall have a Board of Directors to be constituted by Decree of the President of the Republic.

The Board of Directors shall be the prevailing authority in all matters of the Authority, shall discharge its duties, and lay down the general policy that shall be pursued. It may adopt any resolution deemed to be conducive to the achievement of the objectives for which the Authority was created.

By Decree of the President of the Republic, a Deputy Chairman of the Board of Directors of the Authority shall be appointed, who shall act as its Managing Director, and preside over the executive body of the Authority consisting of technical and administrative staff appointed in accordance with the organizational structure approved by the Board of Directors.

The Deputy Chairman of the Board of Directors shall direct the Authority, conduct its business, represent it in litigation and before third parties, and preside over the Board in the Chairman's absence.

The Board of Directors may delegate to the Chairman or to the Deputy Chairman of the Authority part of its duties. The Chairman, Deputy Chairman and principal officers, approved by the Board, shall have the right of signature on behalf of the Authority.

Art. 26. The Authority shall be competent to implement the provisions of this Law, more specifically, to perform the following: i) Study the laws, regulations and resolutions in connection with Arab and foreign investment in the Arab Republic of Egypt and the Free Zones created therein, and submit such proposals as are deemed appropriate in this regard. ii) Prepare lists covering types of activities and projects in the participation of which Arab and foreign capital may be invited. Such lists shall be ratified by the Council of Ministers upon approval by the Authority's Board of Directors. iii) Offer projects for investment by Arab and foreign capital and render advice in connection therewith, familiarize international capital markets and capital exporting countries with the approved lists and the projects offered for Arab and foreign investments plus the conditions and privileges enjoyed by incoming capital when invested within the country and the free zones to be established. iv) Review applications submitted by investors and present the outcome to the Authority's Board of Directors for action thereupon. v) Register incoming capital in terms of the original currency units, if in cash, and also to register and value capital participation in kind or in the form of intangible assets in the light of documents submitted, world prices, and opinion of specialized experts, and to review the valuation of the invested capital at the time of disposal thereof, or liquidation for the purpose of re-exportation or transference abroad. vi) Approve remittance of net profits following examination of the documents which reflect the project's financial position and ascertain, in particular, that all reserves and allocations have been set aside pursuant to laws and standard accounting principles, and also that taxes have been paid upon the expiration of the period of exemption provided in this Law. vii) Facilitate procurement of permits necessary for executing Arab and foreign capital investment projects, including all necessary administrative permits, especially residence permits for businessmen, experts, and foremen recruited overseas for working in projects enjoying the provisions of this Law.

Executive regulations shall determine the rules and procedures under which the Authority shall perform its duties as described in this Law. **viii) To approve projects established with Egyptian capital and owned by Egyptian nationals in accordance with paragraphs (2) and (3) of Article 6 of this Law.**

Art. 27. Applications for investment shall be submitted to the Authority. An application shall specify the amount of capital to be invested, the nature thereof and any other such particulars as shall be required to indicate the structure of the project covered by the application. The Board of Directors of the Authority shall have the authority to approve applications for investment submitted. Such approval shall lapse if the investor shall fail to take serious steps to carry out the project within six months of approval, **unless the Board shall grant renewed approval for such further period as it shall deem fit.**

Art. 28. The Authority shall have a separate budget prepared according to the rules customary in commercial enterprises, unrestricted by the provisions governing the budgets of public authorities and public corporations.

Art. 29. The revenues of the Authority shall consist of the following: i) Credits allocated by the state, ii) Revenues derived from its activities, iii) Charges for services rendered by the Authority. It may receive revenues in free foreign currency pursuant to the rules and regulations adopted by the Board of Directors; and iv) Local or foreign loans when approved according to Law.

CHAPTER FOUR

Free Zones

Art. 30. The Authority's Board of Directors may, upon approval by the Council of Ministers, establish public free zones for the creation of projects authorized under the provisions of this Law. Each public free zone shall have a juridical personality.

By resolution of the Authority's Board of Directors, private free zones may be created exclusively for a single project. In all circumstances, the resolution shall indicate the location and boundaries of the zone.

The establishment of a Free Zone covering an entire city shall be by decree of Law.

Art. 31.   The Authority's Board of Directors is the supreme authority controlling the affairs of the free zones and laying down the general policy to be pursued. The Board may adopt any resolution deemed necessary for the purpose for which such zones have been created, within the limits prescribed by this Law. More specifically it may: i) Coordinate policies and formulate the general planning of free zones in conjunction with the competent administrative authorities. ii) Acquire land, converting it to public or private free zones. iii) Approve budgets and closing accounts of free zones. iv) Assume the functions of the Board of Directors responsible for each public free zone as set forth in Article 33 hereof until the Board of Directors of such public free zone has been constituted, and v) Supervise private free zones until the Board decides to affiliate such private free zones to a public free zone.

Art. 32.   The Authority's Board of Directors shall lay down the executive regulations which govern activities within the free zones from the financial, administrative, and technical aspects, more specifically, as concerns the rules applicable to companies and projects operating within the free zones, and also the rules governing ingress and egress and registration of goods, examination of documents, auditing and controlling, and also policing the zone and collection of leviable dues.

Art. 33.   Each public free zone shall be directed by a Board of Directors which shall be constituted and its Chairman shall be appointed by resolution of the Authority's Board of Directors.

The Board of Directors of the public free zone shall be competent to implement the provisions of this Law and its executive regulations in all matters pertaining to such zone, more specifically the following: i) It shall authorize occupation of lands and real property or rental of real property owned by a third party in the free zone. ii) It shall decide on offers submitted by Arab and foreign investors according to the rules laid down by the Authority's Board of Directors. iii) It shall establish, operate, and exploit stores, warehouses, and areas for shipping, unloading, and warehousing operations. iv) It shall provide instruments and equipment necessary for facilitating operations and projects created within the free zone. v) It shall provide such services as may be needed by the projects created in the free zone in return for charges to be fixed by the Board, and vi) It shall supervise the private free zones affiliated thereto by resolution of the Authority's Board of Directors.

Art. 34.　　Permits for the occupation of free zones or part thereof shall specify the purposes for which they were granted, the validity thereof, and the financial guarantee paid by the licencee. Exemptions and privileges stipulated in this chapter may not be enjoyed except within the limits of the purposes indicated in such licence.

A licence for the occupation of a free zone shall be of a personal nature. The person in whose name a licence is issued may not assign all or part thereof or invite participation by a third party therein unless such is approved by the authority granting the licence.

Art. 35.　　Licences in the free zones may be granted for the performance of the following: i) Storage of transit goods, of indigenous goods on which taxes have been paid and destined for export and foreign goods arriving without import duties, all without prejudice to the law and regulations in force in the Arab Republic of Egypt in connection with goods the circulation of which are prohibited. ii) Sorting, cleaning, mixing, and blending, even with local goods, repacking and similar operations which adapt the condition of goods warehoused in the free zones to the requirements of trade, and processing such goods to meet market requirements. iii) Any manufacturing, assembling, mounting, processing, renewing, or any other operations which need the advantage of a free zone to benefit from the country's geographical position, and iv) Engaging in any trade warranted by the activities within the free zone or intended for the comfort of the employees in the zone.

Art. 36.　　With due regard to provisions in laws and regulations regarding the ban on the circulation of certain goods or materials, goods exported from, or imported into the free zone, shall not be subject to the normal customs procedures applicable to imports and exports nor to customs duties and other taxes and dues, save insofar as is provided for in this Law. Likewise all instruments, machinery, equipment **and transportation equipment** necessary to establishments authorized within such zone shall be exempted from customs duties and other taxes and dues.

The executive regulations of the free zones shall specify the procedures for moving goods from the moment they are unloaded until their arrival at the free zones and vice-versa.

Export and other taxes and duties shall be levied on local goods and materials upon entering the free zone after completion of the export formalities.

The Deputy Chairman of the Board of the Authority or any authorized Chairman of the Board of the public free zones may permit temporary entry of local goods into the free zone for repair or complementary operations thereon, provided that a customs tax shall be exacted in respect of the repair or complementary operation in compliance with customs regulations.

Likewise, the Authority's Deputy Chairman of the Board or any authorized Chairman of the Board of the public free zones may permit temporary entry of free zone goods into the country for repair or complementary operations thereon.

Art. 37. Customs duties and taxes shall be payable in respect of goods withdrawn from the free zone for local consumption, as though such were imported from abroad and in accordance with their condition after manufacturing, with due regard to rules and procedures governing imports. Such customs duties and taxes shall be payable on goods containing **local components,** in proportion to the **ad valorem** value of foreign **components** contained in the manufactured products. **Notwithstanding any of the foregoing, in the event that local components constitute 40% or more of the manufactured product, such dues as shall be payable in accordance with the provisions of this Article shall be reduced by 50%.**

By way of exception from import procedures, the Authority's Deputy Chairman of the Board, or any authorized Chairman of the Board of the public free zones, may permit withdrawal into the country of leftovers, ordinary containers, and empty receptacles after paying the customs duties and taxes due thereon.

He shall have the right to dispose of the above items at the expense of the party concerned should their continued presence in the free zone result in harmful effects on the health or on discipline within the zone.

The Authority's Chairman of the Board or any authorized Chairman of the Board of the public free zones may authorize entry into the country of products not fit for export or scraps resulting from the manufacturing operations within the free zone, provided that the taxes and custom duties are paid thereon, on condition that no competition with national industries results.

Art. 38. Goods entering the free zone shall be subject to no restriction as to the duration of their stay therein, nor shall imports into or exports from the free zone be subject to any import or export restriction.

Art. 39. Employees of the Authority and free zones appointed by resolution of the Minister of Justice on the basis of a request from the Authority's Chairman of the Board shall possess the capacity of judicial officers within the limits of their functions. The Authority's Deputy Chairman of the Board, or any person so authorized, may request the Public Prosecutor to authorize the judicial officers to inspect any part of the free zone or conduct investigations, whenever such is warranted.

Art. 40. By exception to the provisions of Law No. 66 of 1963, enacting the Customs Code, the Customs Administration shall advise the Chairman of the Board of the free zone of any cases of unaccounted shortage or surplus in the goods manifested in the bills of lading, whether in the number of packages or their contents or packed or loose goods if consigned to the free zone.

Responsibility for the cases specified in the preceding paragraph and percentages of allowances shall be regulated by resolution of the Authority's Board of Directors.

Art. 41. Those authorized to operate under the provisions of this Chapter shall be liable for procuring insurance coverage for buildings, equipment, and machinery against all hazards. They shall also be bound to remove same at their own expense within such period as may be fixed by the Chairman of the Board of the free zone calculated from the date of expiration of their licences, unless the Board of the free zone elects to purchase same therefrom.

Art. 42. Entry into and residence in the free zones, as well as the introduction of Egyptian currency into and its withdrawal from the free zones, shall be in conformity with the conditions and terms to be set forth in the executive regulations.

The regulations shall also fix the charges for occupying areas in which goods are deposited.

Art. 43. Marine transport projects established in the free zones shall be exempted from the conditions concerning the nationality of the ship owner and crew stipulated in the Merchant Marine code and in Law No. 84 of 1949, in connection with the registration of vessels. Likewise, they will be exempted from the provisions of Law No. 12 for 1964, establishing the Egyptian General Corporation for Maritime Transport.

Art. 44. The free zones shall be subject to the provisions of Egyptian legislation where no special provision is made in this Law, more particularly the legislation governing health quarantine procedures, health fees, and protection of plants against epidemics and parasites. The Authority's Board of Directors shall lay down the implementing rules for the application of the provisions of such legislation within the free zone.

Art. 45. Disputes arising between projects established in free zones, or arising between such projects and the Authority or any other authorities or administrative bodies connected with the business activities within the zone, may be submitted, by agreement, to arbitration.

An Arbitration Board shall be constituted to decide on the dispute in accordance with the rules and pursuant to the measures stipulated in Article 8 hereof.

The Arbitration Board may also examine disputes arising between projects existing in the free zone and natural or juridical persons, whether indigenous or alien, if such persons agree to refer the dispute to the Arbitration Board before or after it arises.

Art. 46. Without prejudice to the provisions of this Law, projects established in the free zone, and dividends thereof, shall be exempted from the provisions of tax and duty laws in the Arab Republic of Egypt. Arab and foreign funds invested **in the free zones shall likewise be exempted from inheritance taxes and death duties.**

Nevertheless, such projects shall be subject to dues payable for services and to an annual duty **not exceeding one percent (1%)** of the value of goods entering or leaving the free zone for the account of the project. Such annual duty shall be determined by resolution of the Authority's Board of Directors. Trade in transit goods shall be exempt from such a fee.

Likewise, projects, the main activities of which do not require ingress or egress of commodities, shall be subject to an annual duty determined by the Board of Directors of the Authority, with due consideration for the nature and volume of activities and not exceeding three percent (3%) of the annual value added of the project.

Art. 47. Payments subject to tax on income, such as wages, salaries, compensations and the like, paid by projects existing within the free zones to their expatriate employees shall be exempted from the general tax on income.

Art. 48. Provisions of Articles 6 and 7 of this Law shall apply to the capital authorized to operate in the free zone.

Art. 49. Transactions carried out in the free zone or between such zones and other countries shall not be subject to the provisions of exchange control Laws.

Art. 50. Companies with activities in the free zones shall not be subject to the rules stipulated in Laws No. 26 of 1954 and No. 73 of 1973 referred to above. Statutes of the companies created in the free zones shall be patterned after the model formulated by the Council of Ministers on the basis of a proposal by the Authority's Board of Directors. The statutes of such companies shall be enacted by decree of the President of the Republic and shall enjoy a juridical personality from the date of publication of their statutes and Articles of Incorporation.

The above provision shall apply to any amendment in company statutes.

Art. 51.   Provisions of Law No. 173 of 1958, requiring an Egyptian to obtain a permit from the competent authorities prior to taking up employment with foreign organisations shall not apply to Egyptian employees engaged by projects and establishments enjoying the provisions of this Chapter.

Art. 52.   No employment may be taken up in the free zone except after obtaining a permit from the zone's Chairman of the Board under such terms and conditions as are specified in the executive regulation of the free zones and upon payment of a fee to be fixed in such regulation with a maximum of five hundred Egyptian pounds annually.

Art. 53.   Contracts of Employment concluded with employees of Egyptian nationality shall be drawn in triplicate in the Arabic language, each party retaining a copy thereof and the third copy to be deposited with the Administration of the free zone. Contracts shall specify the type of work, duration thereof, and agreed wage.

A translation of said Contract may be appended in a foreign language.

The employer shall file with the Administration of the free zone a copy translated into English or French of the contracts of Employment concluded with expatriate employees within one week from the date the employee takes up employment.

Art. 54.   Projects established in the free zone shall develop opportunities and prepare appropriate training programs for the training of employees having Egyptian nationality in order that they may become skilled labor.

Art. 55.   The Executive Regulations shall lay down, as the minimum level required, the rules applying to employees in the projects authorized to operate in the free zones, more specifically the following: i) Fixing the proportion of employees having Egyptian nationality. ii) Fixing the minimum wages provided they do not fall below the minimum wages applicable in the Arab Republic of Egypt. iii) Fixing daily hours of work and weekly holidays, provided the hours of work may not exceed 42 hours per week. iv) Fixing overtime and dues therefor. v) Specifying the social and medical services rendered by the enterprises to their employees and the necessary precautions to protect them during work. vi) Specifying the length of all kinds of vacations and wages payable in lieu thereof. vii) Specifying the general principles of discipline, discharge, and compensation of employees.

Art. 56. Employees in projects performing activities in the free zones and with Egyptian nationality shall be subject to the provisions of the social insurance laws, unless the enterprise guarantees a superior insurance system approved by the General Organization for Social Insurance.

Art. 57. Without prejudice to any more severe penalty provided in any other Law, violation of Article 42 and 52 of the provisions of this Law shall be punishable by imprisonment for a term not exceeding six months or a fine not less than five pounds and not exceeding two hundred pounds or both penalties.

Any person violating any other provisions contained in this Law or in the Supplementary Regulation of the free zones shall be liable to a fine of not less than five pounds and not exceeding one hundred pounds.

No legal action may be brought in respect of the violations referred to in the preceding two paragraphs except upon request of the Authority's Chairman of the Board or any person authorized thereby. The Authority's Board of Directors or any authorized person appointed thereby may, in the course of litigation, effect conciliation as regards fines prescribed in this Law.

All fines ruled by a court in respect of offences against the provisions of this Law or paid by the violator by way of conciliation shall revert to the Authority.

ANNEX A

Law No. 32 of 1977 Amending Certain Provisions of Law No. 43 of 1974 Concerning the Investment of Arab and Foreign Funds and the Free Zones.

In The Name Of The People

The President Of The Republic

The People's Assembly has approved and issued the following law:
[The provisions of Articles 1—4 have been incorporated in the preceding revised text of Law No. 43 of 1974, as amended by Law No. 32 of 1977].

Art. 5. In the event that invested capital has already been transferred in part or in full to the Arab Republic of Egypt at the official rate according to the provisions of Law No. 43 of 1974, such capital may either, upon the agreement of the partners representing three fourths of the invested capital, or by a decision of a special shareholders' meeting, to the extent of the amount so transferred, be revalued within the limits of the amounts transferred according to the provisions of Article 2 bis of the said Law; in such case the project may increase the value of its shares or issue non-voting bonus shares in an amount equivalent to the difference resulting from the revaluation. Any such revaluation and issuance of shares shall be accomplished free of any taxes or fees. In the event that revaluation does not take place as authorized above, the value of the shares or the value of the amount that has been transferred, as the case may be, shall remain calculated at the official rate of exchange at which the transfer took place. Thus, the proportion of participation in the profits as determined by that value when the project was approved shall remain the same without change thereon. Profits resulting from these shares, or from the amount that has been transferred thereof, as the case may be, shall be distributed in accordance with the proportion of participation based on such original valuation.

Art. 6. The Minister of Economy and Economic Cooperation shall issue, upon proposal of the Board of Directors of the Authority, Model Articles of Incorporation for Joint Stock Companies and Limited Liability Companies for joint ventures established according to the provisions of this Law whether inland or in Free Zones. Project owners are not obliged to follow such Model Articles, insofar as their provisions do not relate to Egyptian public policy. Also, the principal Bylaws of Joint Stock Companies established, whether in-land or in Free Zones, under the provisions of this Law, shall be issued by decree of the Minister of Economy and Economic Cooperation.

Art. 7. All provisions of any law conflicting with the provisions of the said Law No. 43 of 1974 shall be repealed.

Art. 8. This Law shall be published in the Official Gazette and shall come into force from the date of its publication.

This Law is stamped with the State Seal and is executed as one of its Laws.

Signature of the President
5 June, 1977.

Published in the Official Gazette on June 9, 1977.

BIBLIOGRAPHY

GENERAL

Books

Baranson, Jack. *Industrial Technologies for Developing Economies.* New York: Frederick A. Praeger, 1969.

Carr, David W. *Foreign Investment and Development in the Southwest Pacific: With Special Reference to Australia and Indonesia.* New York: Praeger Special Studies, 1978.

Chudson, Walter A. *The International Transfer of Commercial Technology to Developing Countries,* UNITAR Research Reports No. 13. United Nations Institute for Training and Research, 1971.

Dunning, John H. "Technology, United States Investment and European Economic Growth." In *The International Corporation: A Symposium,* edited by Charles P. Kindleberger. Cambridge, MA: The MIT Press, 1970.

Fforde, J. S. *An International Trade in Managerial Skills.* Oxford: Basil Blackwell, 1957.

Haberler, Gottfried, and Robert M. Stern, ed. *Equilibrium and Growth in the World Economy, Economic Essays By Ragnar Nurkse.* Cambridge: Harvard University Press, 1962.

Mikesell, Raymond F., ed. *U.S. Private and Government Investment Abroad.* Eugene: University of Oregon Press, 1962.

Svennilson, Ingvar: "The Transfer of Industrial Know-How to Non-Industrialized Countries." In Kenneth Berrill, ed., *Economic Development with Special Reference to East Asia.* New York: St. Martins Press, 1964.

United Nations Department of Economic and Social Affairs. *The Impact of Multinational Corporations on Development and on International Relations.* New York: United Nations, 1974.

Vernon, Raymond. *Sovereignty at Bay—The Multinational Spread of U.S. Enterprises.* New York: Basic Books, 1971.

Periodicals

Baranson, Jack. "Transfer of Technical Knowledge by International Corporations to Developing Economies," *American Economic Review* 56 (1966): 259–67, 275–77.

Caves, Richard. "International Corporations: The Industrial Economics of Foreign Investment." *Economica* 38 (1971): 1–27.

Quinn, James Brian. "Technology Transfer by Multinational Companies." *Harvard Business Review* 47 (1969): 147–61.

Robertson, Dennis. "The Future of International Trade." *Economic Journal* 48 (1938): 1–17.

Safarian, A. E. "Perspectives on Foreign Direct Investment from the Viewpoint of a Capital Receiving Country." *The Journal of Finance* 28 (1973): 419–38.

EGYPT

Books

Agency for International Development. *U.S. Economic Assistance to Egypt—A Report of a Special Interagency Task Force.* Washington, D.C.: February 1978.

Ahmad, Yusuf J. *Absorptive Capacity of the Egyptian Economy.* Paris: Development Center of the Organization for Economic Cooperation and Development, 1976.

Arthur D. Little, Inc., *An Assessment of Egypt's Industrial Sector,* Report to the Special Interagency Task Force Reviewing the U.S. Security Supporting Assistance Program for Egypt. Cambridge, MA: January 1978.

Barbour, K. M. *The Growth, Location and Structure of Industry in Egypt.* New York: Praeger Publishers, 1972.

Business International. *Egypt, Business Gateway to the Middle East.* New York: Business International, 1976.

Driscoll, Robert E., P. F. Hayek, Farouk A. Zaki. *Foreign Investment in Egypt: An Analysis of Critical Factors with Emphasis on the Foreign Investment Code.* New York: Fund for Multinational Management Education, 1978.

Egypt-U.S. Business Council. *Report on Foreign Investment in Egypt.* Washington, D.C.: 1976.

Fahmy, Moustafa. *La Revolution de l'Industrie en Egypte et Ses Consequences Sociales au 19ᵉ Siecle (1800–1850).* Leiden: E. J. Brill, 1954.

Federation of Egyptian Industries. *Year Book 1969, 1972 and 1975.* Cairo: General Organization for Government Printing Office, 1969, 1972, and 1975.

Government of Egypt. *Egypt's Industrial Revolution in 20 Years 1952–1972.* Cairo, 1973.

Hansen, Bent, and Karim Nashashibi. *Foreign Trade Regimes and Economic Development: Egypt.* New York: National Bureau of Economic Research, Columbia U. Press, 1975.

Harbison, Frederick. *Human Resources for Egyptian Enterprise.* New York: McGraw Hill Book Co., Inc., 1958.

Issawi, Charles. *Egypt in Revolution—An Economic Analysis.* New York: Oxford University Press, 1963.

El-Kammash, Mazdi. *Economic Development and Planning in Egypt.* New York: Praeger Special Studies, 1968.

Mabro, Robert, and Samir Radwan. *The Industrialization of Egypt 1939–1973—Policy and Performance.* New York: Oxford University Press, 1976.

Mead, Donald C. *Growth and Structural Change in the Egyptian Economy.* Homewood, Illinois: Richard D. Irwin, 1967.

Ministry of Planning, Government of Egypt. *Draft Five-Year Plan, 1978–82.* Cairo: 1977.

Nyrop, Richard F. *Area Handbook for Egypt.* Washington, D.C.: Foreign Area Studies, 1976.

O'Brien, Patrick. *The Revolution in Egypt's Economic System.* New York: Oxford University Press, 1966.

Roy, Delwin A. *Private Industry Sector Development in Egypt: An Analysis of Trends, 1973-1977.* Report to the Special Interagency Task Force Reviewing the U.S. Security Supporting Assistance Program for Egypt. Washington, D.C.: AID, January 1978.

Stephens, John W., and P. F. Hayek. *Investment in Egypt: Law No. 43 and Its Implications for the Transfer of Technology.* New York: Fund for Multinational Management Education, 1974.

Suez Canal Authority. *Annual Report, 1959; 1960.* Cairo, 1960 and 1961.

U.S. Department of State-American Embassy, Cairo. *Foreign Economic Trends—Egypt.* Washington, D.C., August 1978.

Periodicals

"Achievements of the Industrial and Mining Sector in Egypt during 1974." National Bank of Egypt, *Economic Bulletin* (1975): 388–97.

Deeb, Marius. "Bank Misr and the Emergence of the National Bourgeoisie in Egypt." *Middle Eastern Studies* 12 (1976): 69–86.

"Domestic Economic Developments—1976." National Bank of Egypt, *Economic Bulletin* (1977): 129–51.

"Evolution of Exchange Control in Egypt with Special Reference to Law No. 97/1976." National Bank of Egypt, *Economic Bulletin* (1977): 10–18.

"Follow-Up and Appraisal of Economic and Social Growth in Egypt during 1974." National Bank of Egypt, *Economic Bulletin* (1975): 369–87.

"Follow-Up of Egypt's Economic and Social Development during 1975." National Bank of Egypt, *Economic Bulletin* (1976): 262–67.

"Follow-Up of the 1976 State Plan." National Bank of Egypt, *Economic Bulletin* (1977): 247–55.

"Foreign Banks Move In." *Financial Times* (July 31, 1978).

Gray, Albert L., Jr. "Egypt's Ten Year Economic Plan 1973–82." *Middle East Journal* 30 (1976): 36–48.

Issawi, Charles. "Egypt Since 1800: A Study in Lopsided Development." *The Journal of Economic History* 31 (1961): 1–27.

McCarthy, Justin A. "Nineteenth Century Egyptian Population." *Middle Eastern Studies* 12 (1976): 1–39.

McKay, Arnold. "U.S. Investors Fail to Rush Into Egypt," "Program to Stir U.S. Investment in Egypt Generally in Limbo," and "U.S. Investment in Egypt May Grow," *Journal of Commerce,* March 27, 28, 29, 1978.

"The National Economy—1977." National Bank of Egypt, *Economic Bulletin* (1978): 10–21.

"1977 Draft Economic and Social Development Plan." National Bank of Egypt, *Economic Bulletin* (1977): 256–67.

"Ominous Signs On the Farm." *Financial Times* (July 31, 1978).

Overseas Private Investment Corporation. "Investment Climate: Clearing and Warmer," "Law No. 43: The New Legal Framework For Investment," and "1-Stop Shopping." *Spotlites* (December 1974).

"Progress Report Regarding 'Open-Door' Policy Projects in Egypt as at the End of 1976." National Bank of Egypt, *Economic Bulletin* (1977): 152–161.

"Shipping Returns to Suez." *Financial Times* (July 31, 1978).

"Steady Income From Oil." *Financial Times* (July 31, 1978).

"Suez Canal For All Ages." *Financial Times* (July 31, 1978).

Taylor, Lance, "The Political Economy of Egypt: An Opening to What?" *Middle East Review* (Summer 1978), pp. 10–15.

Tignor, Robert L. "The Egyptian Revolution of 1919: New Directions in the Egyptian Economy." *Middle Eastern Studies* 12 (1976): 41–67.

"Vast Tourism Potential." *Financial Times* (July 31, 1978).

ABOUT THE AUTHOR

DAVID WILLIAM CARR is Assistant Program Economist at the United States Agency for International Development Mission at Damascus, Syria. Until 1979, he was Director of the Pacific-Asia and Middle East/Africa Divisions of the National Foreign Trade Council in New York City. Before 1969, he served as Economic Officer and Commercial Attaché for the State Department Foreign Service in Jordan, Lebanon, Aden, and Saudi Arabia.

During 1978, Mr. Carr published for Praeger Special Studies a book titled, *Foreign Investment and Development in the Southwest Pacific: With Special Reference to Australia and Indonesia.*

Mr. Carr holds a B.A. from Princeton University, an M.A. from the Fletcher School of Law and Diplomacy, and a Ph.D. from New York University.